EYEWITNESS VISUAL DICTIONARIES

THE VISUAL
DICTIONARY *of*
CARS

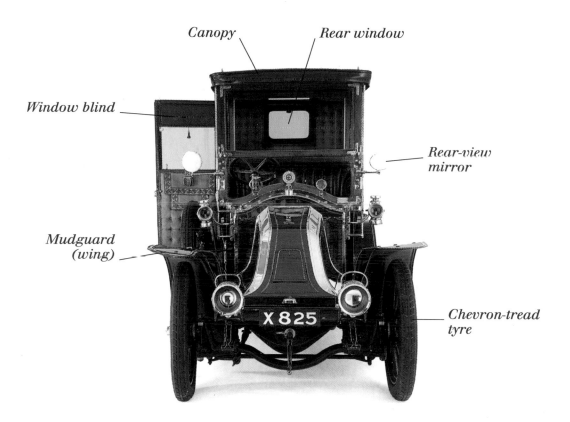

Canopy

Rear window

Window blind

Rear-view mirror

Mudguard (wing)

Chevron-tread tyre

X 825

FRONT VIEW OF 1906 RENAULT

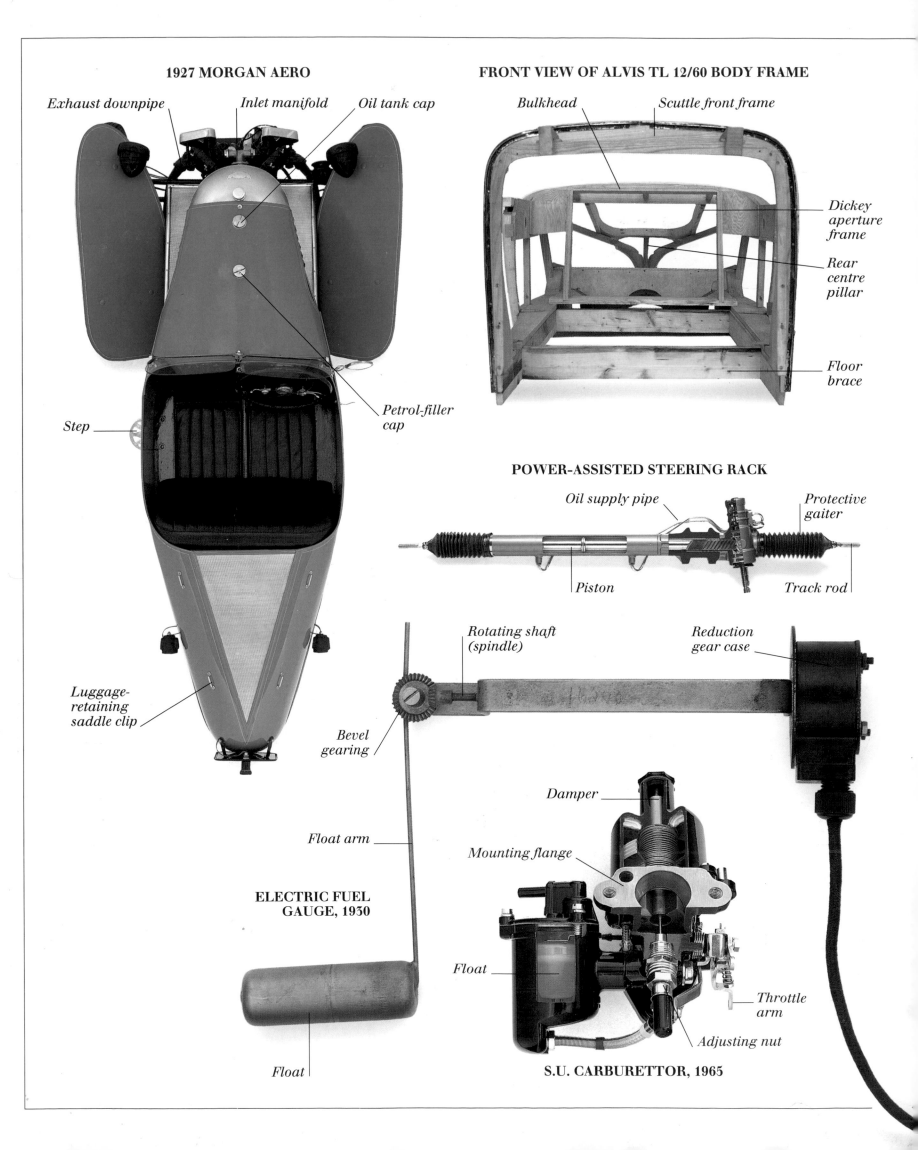

1927 MORGAN AERO

Exhaust downpipe

Inlet manifold

Oil tank cap

Step

Petrol-filler cap

Luggage-retaining saddle clip

FRONT VIEW OF ALVIS TL 12/60 BODY FRAME

Bulkhead

Scuttle front frame

Dickey aperture frame

Rear centre pillar

Floor brace

POWER-ASSISTED STEERING RACK

Oil supply pipe

Protective gaiter

Piston

Track rod

Rotating shaft (spindle)

Reduction gear case

Bevel gearing

Float arm

Damper

Mounting flange

Float

Throttle arm

Adjusting nut

ELECTRIC FUEL GAUGE, 1930

Float

S.U. CARBURETTOR, 1965

EYEWITNESS VISUAL DICTIONARIES

THE VISUAL
DICTIONARY *of*
CARS

Indicator needle

PETROL

0 2 4 6 8 10 12 14 FULL

GALLONS

Drive cable

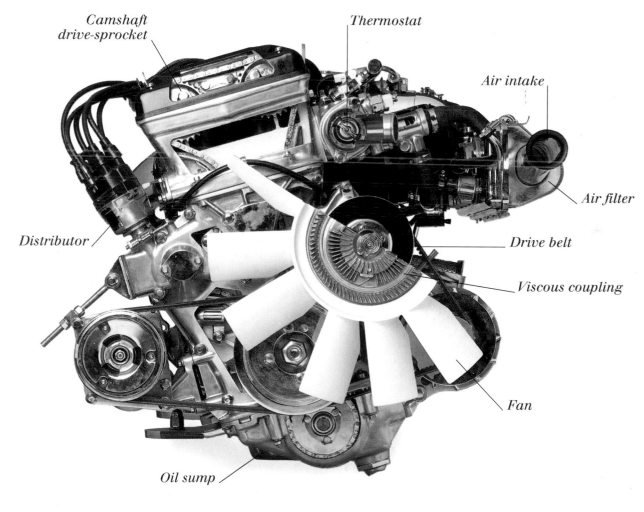

Camshaft drive-sprocket

Thermostat

Air intake

Air filter

Distributor

Drive belt

Viscous coupling

Fan

Oil sump

FRONT VIEW OF A JAGUAR STRAIGHT 6 ENGINE

DORLING KINDERSLEY

LONDON • NEW YORK • STUTTGART

A DORLING KINDERSLEY BOOK

PROJECT ART EDITOR NICOLA LIDDIARD
DESIGNER PAUL CALVER

PROJECT EDITOR PAUL DOCHERTY
CONSULTANT EDITOR DAVID BURGESS-WISE

SERIES ART EDITOR STEPHEN KNOWLDEN
SERIES EDITOR MARTYN PAGE
ART DIRECTOR CHEZ PICTHALL
MANAGING EDITOR RUTH MIDGLEY

PHOTOGRAPHY SIMON CLAY, JOHN LEPINE, TIM RIDLEY, DAVE RUDKIN
ILLUSTRATIONS MICK GILLAH

PRODUCTION HILARY STEPHENS

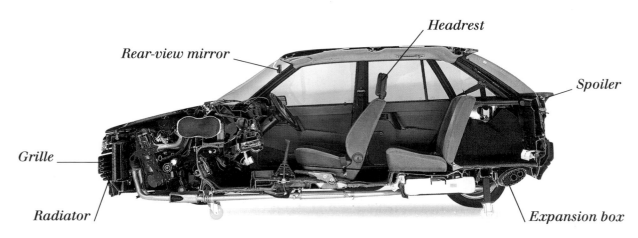

Headrest

Rear-view mirror

Spoiler

Grille

Radiator

Expansion box

SECTIONED SEAT IBIZA

FIRST PUBLISHED IN GREAT BRITAIN IN 1992
BY DORLING KINDERSLEY LIMITED,
9 HENRIETTA STREET, LONDON WC2E 8PS

A CIP CATALOGUE RECORD FOR THIS BOOK IS AVAILABLE FROM THE BRITISH LIBRARY

ISBN 0-86318-835-4

REPRODUCED BY COLOURSCAN, SINGAPORE
PRINTED AND BOUND BY ARNOLDO MONDADORI, VERONA, ITALY

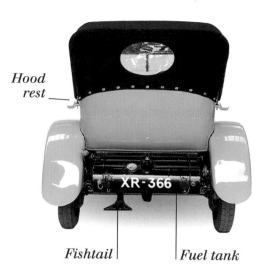

Folding windscreen

Honeycomb radiator

Beam axle

1913 ROLLS ROYCE SILVER GHOST TOURER

Contents

Hood rest

Fishtail

Fuel tank

1924 ROLLS ROYCE SILVER GHOST TOURER

Gearbox

Fuel tank

1932 15/18 HP LANCHESTER RUNNING CHASSIS

Backrest release

Seat belt

Runner

COMPUTERIZED ELECTRIC SEAT

Canvas tyre

Felloe

Spoke

Hub

ARTILLERY WHEEL (WOODEN-SPOKED WHEEL)

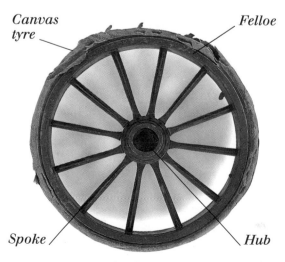

Calorimeter

Radiator cap

Radiator badge

ALFA ROMEO RADIATOR AND GRILLE

The first cars

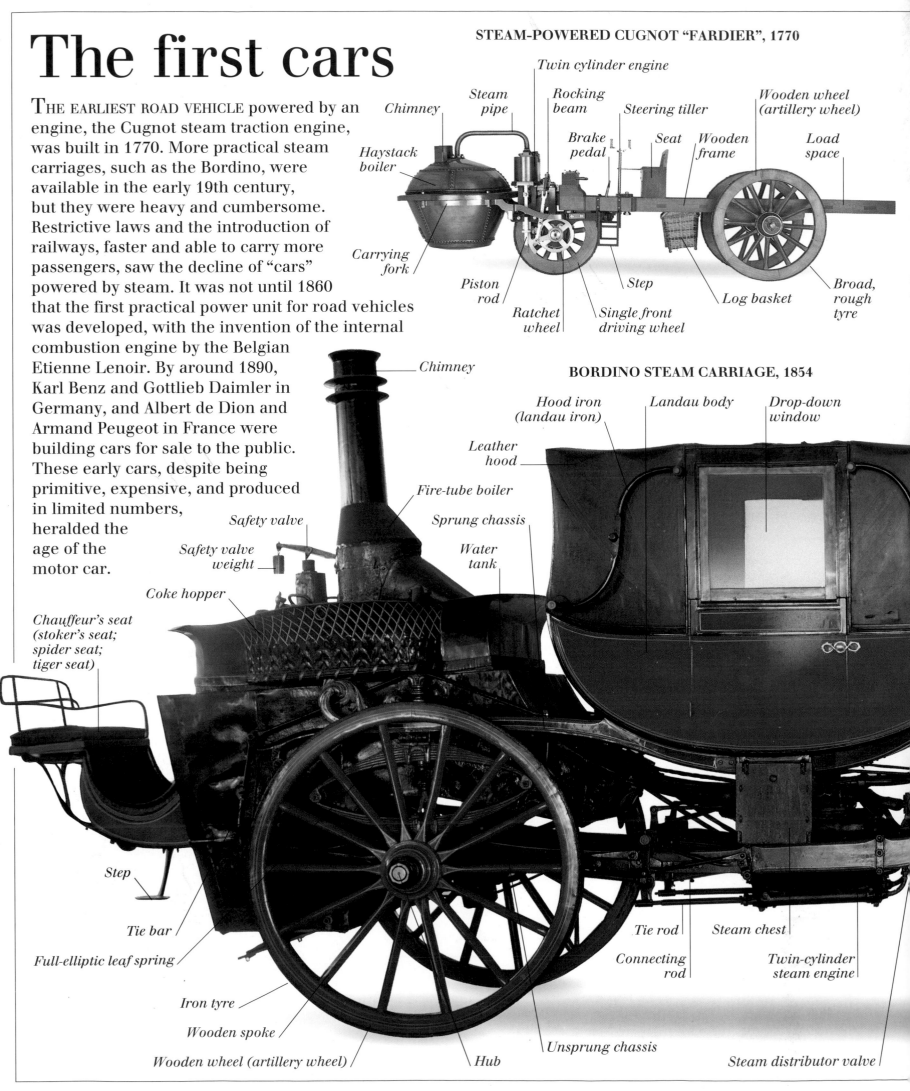

THE EARLIEST ROAD VEHICLE powered by an engine, the Cugnot steam traction engine, was built in 1770. More practical steam carriages, such as the Bordino, were available in the early 19th century, but they were heavy and cumbersome. Restrictive laws and the introduction of railways, faster and able to carry more passengers, saw the decline of "cars" powered by steam. It was not until 1860 that the first practical power unit for road vehicles was developed, with the invention of the internal combustion engine by the Belgian Etienne Lenoir. By around 1890, Karl Benz and Gottlieb Daimler in Germany, and Albert de Dion and Armand Peugeot in France were building cars for sale to the public. These early cars, despite being primitive, expensive, and produced in limited numbers, heralded the age of the motor car.

STEAM-POWERED CUGNOT "FARDIER", 1770

Twin cylinder engine

Chimney

Steam pipe

Rocking beam

Steering tiller

Wooden wheel (artillery wheel)

Haystack boiler

Brake pedal

Seat

Wooden frame

Load space

Carrying fork

Piston rod

Ratchet wheel

Single front driving wheel

Step

Log basket

Broad, rough tyre

BORDINO STEAM CARRIAGE, 1854

Chimney

Hood iron (landau iron)

Landau body

Drop-down window

Leather hood

Fire-tube boiler

Sprung chassis

Safety valve

Water tank

Safety valve weight

Coke hopper

Chauffeur's seat (stoker's seat; spider seat; tiger seat)

Step

Tie bar

Full-elliptic leaf spring

Iron tyre

Wooden spoke

Wooden wheel (artillery wheel)

Hub

Unsprung chassis

Tie rod

Connecting rod

Steam chest

Twin-cylinder steam engine

Steam distributor valve

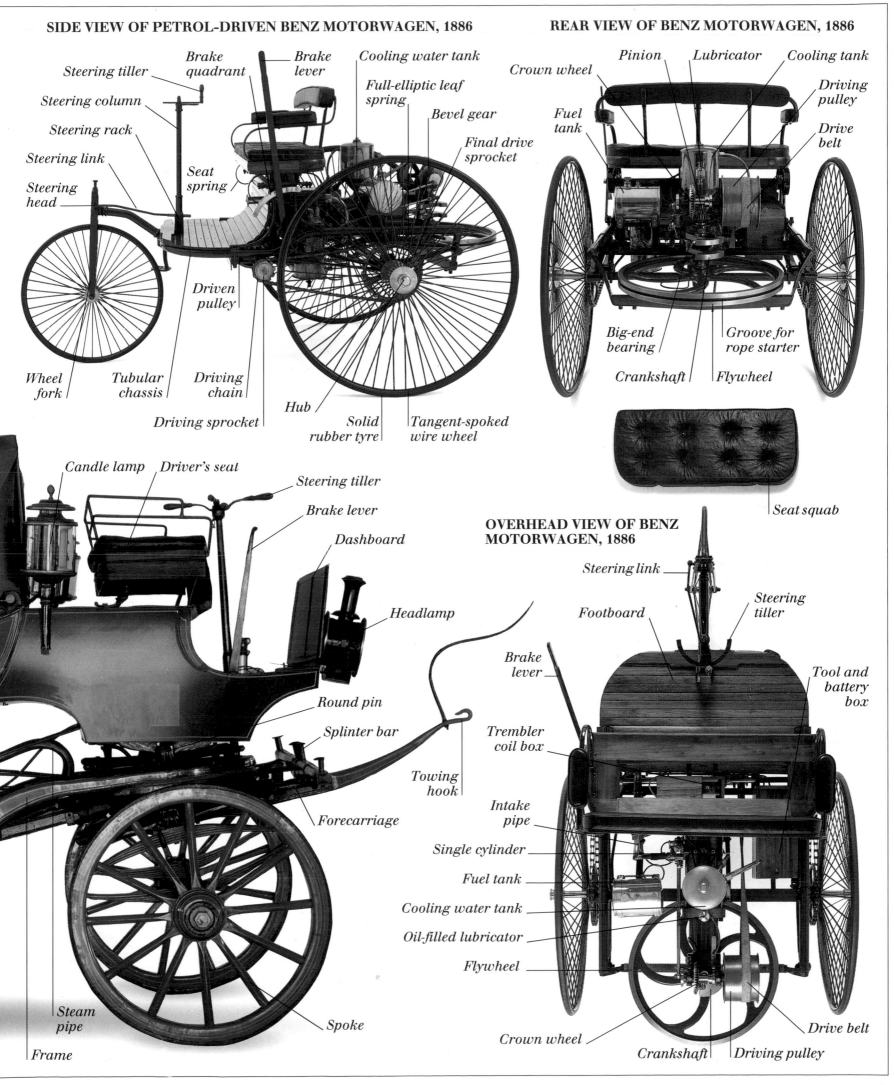

SIDE VIEW OF PETROL-DRIVEN BENZ MOTORWAGEN, 1886

Steering tiller
Brake quadrant
Brake lever
Cooling water tank
Full-elliptic leaf spring
Bevel gear
Steering column
Steering rack
Steering link
Final drive sprocket
Steering head
Seat spring
Driven pulley
Wheel fork
Tubular chassis
Driving chain
Driving sprocket
Hub
Solid rubber tyre
Tangent-spoked wire wheel

REAR VIEW OF BENZ MOTORWAGEN, 1886

Crown wheel
Pinion
Lubricator
Cooling tank
Driving pulley
Fuel tank
Drive belt
Big-end bearing
Groove for rope starter
Crankshaft
Flywheel
Seat squab

OVERHEAD VIEW OF BENZ MOTORWAGEN, 1886

Steering link
Footboard
Steering tiller
Brake lever
Tool and battery box
Trembler coil box
Intake pipe
Single cylinder
Fuel tank
Cooling water tank
Oil-filled lubricator
Flywheel
Crown wheel
Crankshaft
Driving pulley
Drive belt

Candle lamp
Driver's seat
Steering tiller
Brake lever
Dashboard
Headlamp
Round pin
Splinter bar
Towing hook
Forecarriage
Steam pipe
Frame
Spoke

Elegance and utility

DURING THE FIRST DECADE OF THIS CENTURY, the motorist who could afford it had a choice of some of the finest cars ever made. These handbuilt cars were powerful and luxurious, using the finest woods, leathers, and cloths, and bodywork made to the customer's individual requirements; some had six-cylinder engines as big as 15 litres. The price of such cars was several times that of an average house, and their yearly running costs were also very high. As a result, basic, utilitarian cars became popular. Costing perhaps one-tenth of the price of a luxury car, these cars had very little trim and often had only single-cylinder engines.

1904 OLDSMOBILE SINGLE-CYLINDER ENGINE

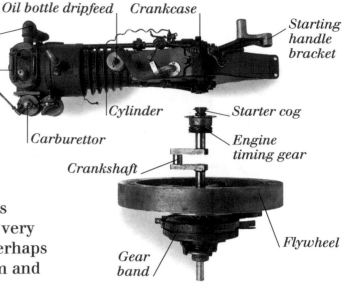

Oil bottle dripfeed
Crankcase
Starting handle bracket
Exhaust pipe
Cylinder head
Carburettor
Cylinder
Starter cog
Engine timing gear
Crankshaft
Flywheel
Gear band

FRONT VIEW OF 1906 RENAULT

SIDE VIEW OF 1906 RENAULT

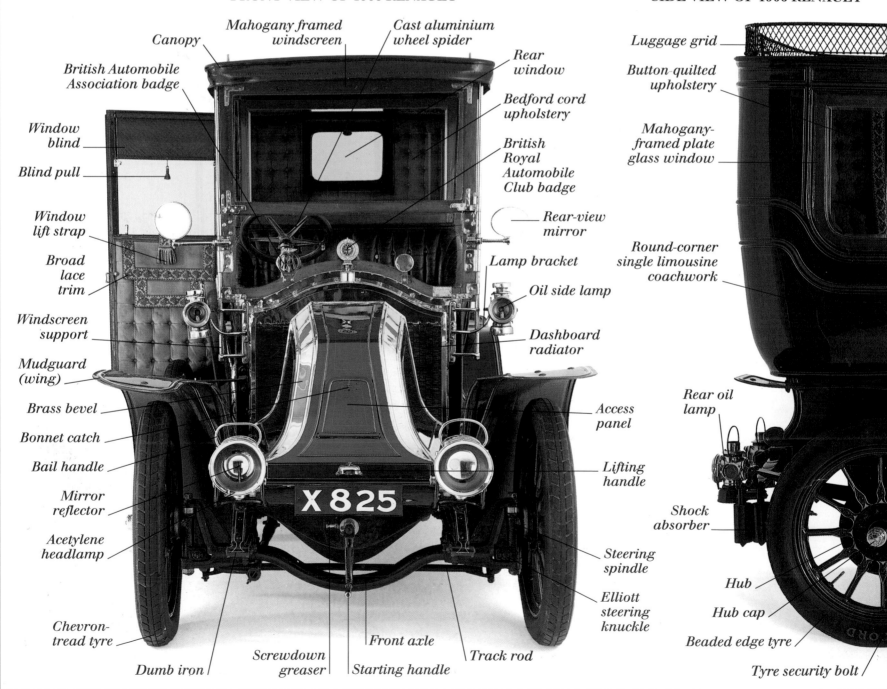

Canopy
Mahogany framed windscreen
Cast aluminium wheel spider
Rear window
British Automobile Association badge
Bedford cord upholstery
British Royal Automobile Club badge
Window blind
Blind pull
Window lift strap
Rear-view mirror
Broad lace trim
Lamp bracket
Windscreen support
Oil side lamp
Mudguard (wing)
Dashboard radiator
Brass bevel
Bonnet catch
Access panel
Bail handle
Lifting handle
Mirror reflector
Acetylene headlamp
X 825
Steering spindle
Elliott steering knuckle
Chevron-tread tyre
Dumb iron
Screwdown greaser
Front axle
Starting handle
Track rod

Luggage grid
Button-quilted upholstery
Mahogany-framed plate glass window
Round-corner single limousine coachwork
Rear oil lamp
Shock absorber
Hub
Hub cap
Beaded edge tyre
Tyre security bolt

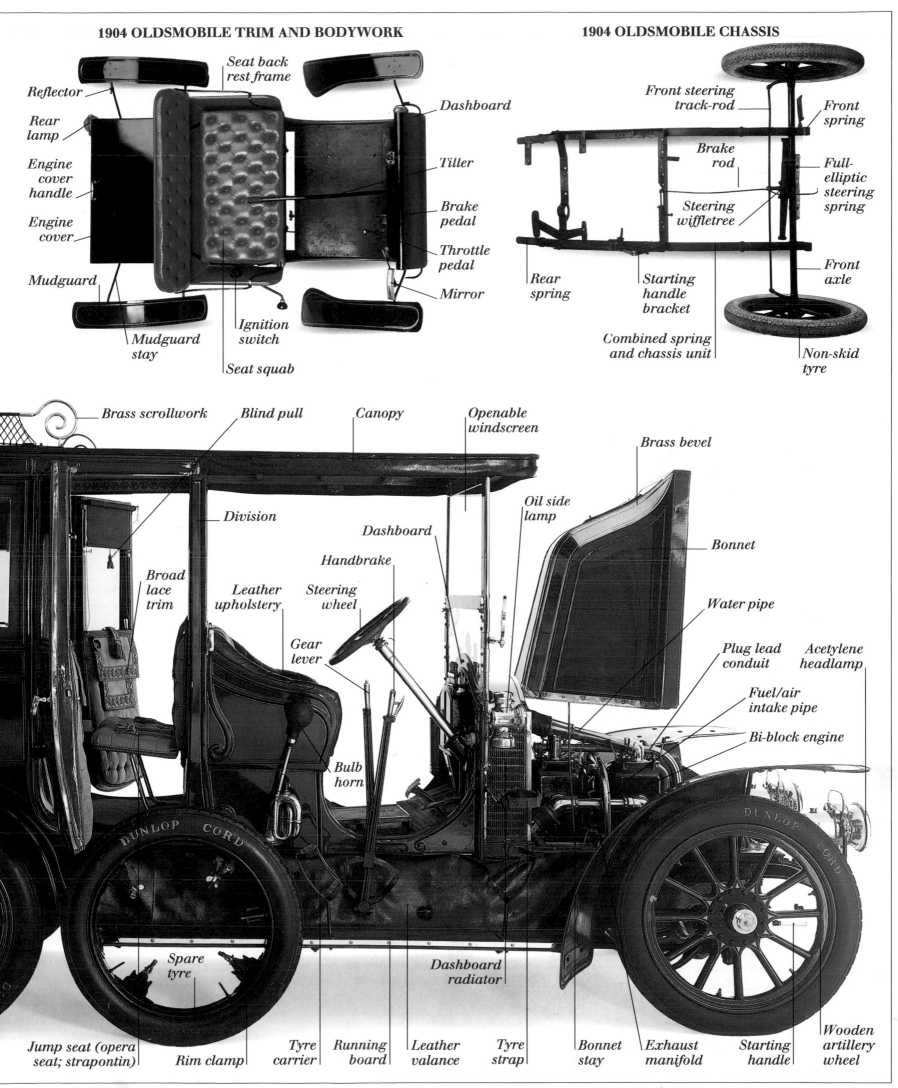

1904 OLDSMOBILE TRIM AND BODYWORK

Reflector
Rear lamp
Engine cover handle
Engine cover
Mudguard
Mudguard stay
Ignition switch
Seat squab
Seat back rest frame
Dashboard
Tiller
Brake pedal
Throttle pedal
Mirror

1904 OLDSMOBILE CHASSIS

Front steering track-rod
Front spring
Brake rod
Full-elliptic steering spring
Steering wiffletree
Rear spring
Starting handle bracket
Front axle
Combined spring and chassis unit
Non-skid tyre

Brass scrollwork
Blind pull
Canopy
Openable windscreen
Brass bevel
Division
Oil side lamp
Dashboard
Bonnet
Broad lace trim
Leather upholstery
Handbrake
Steering wheel
Water pipe
Gear lever
Plug lead conduit
Acetylene headlamp
Fuel/air intake pipe
Bi-block engine
Bulb horn
Jump seat (opera seat; strapontin)
Rim clamp
Spare tyre
Tyre carrier
Running board
Leather valance
Dashboard radiator
Tyre strap
Bonnet stay
Exhaust manifold
Starting handle
Wooden artillery wheel

Mass-production

THE FIRST CARS WERE HAND-ASSEMBLED from individually built parts, a time-consuming procedure that required skilled mechanics and made cars very expensive. This problem was solved, in America, by a Detroit car manufacturer named Henry Ford; he introduced mass-production by using standardized parts, and later combined these with a moving production line. The work was brought to the workers, each of whom performed one simple task in the construction process as the chassis moved along the line. The first mass-produced car, the Ford Model T, was launched in 1908 and was available in a limited range of body styles and colours. However, when the production line was introduced in 1914, the colour range was cut back; the Model T became available, as Henry Ford said, in "any colour you like, so long as it's black". Ford cut the production time for a car from several days to about 12 hours, and eventually to minutes, making cars much cheaper than before. As a result, by 1920 half the cars in the world were Model T Fords.

FRONT VIEW OF 1913 FORD MODEL T

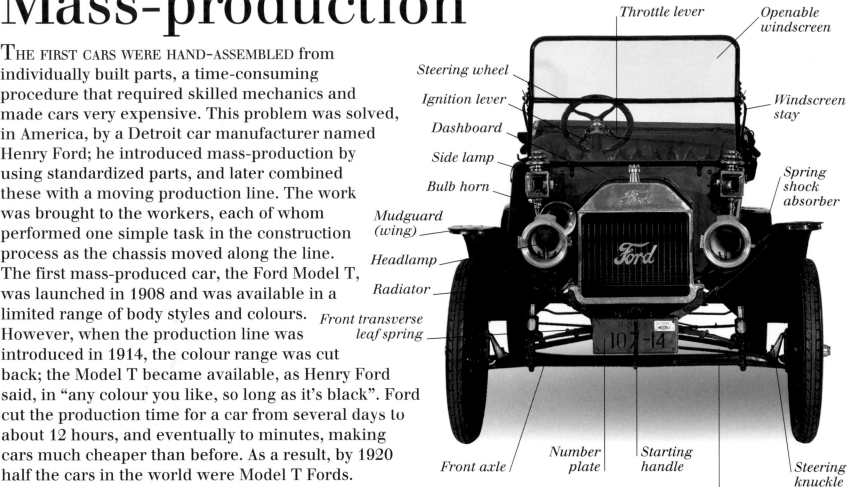

Throttle lever
Openable windscreen
Steering wheel
Ignition lever
Windscreen stay
Dashboard
Side lamp
Bulb horn
Spring shock absorber
Mudguard (wing)
Headlamp
Radiator
Front transverse leaf spring
Number plate
Starting handle
Front axle
Steering knuckle
Steering spindle connecting-rod

STAGES OF FORD MODEL T PRODUCTION

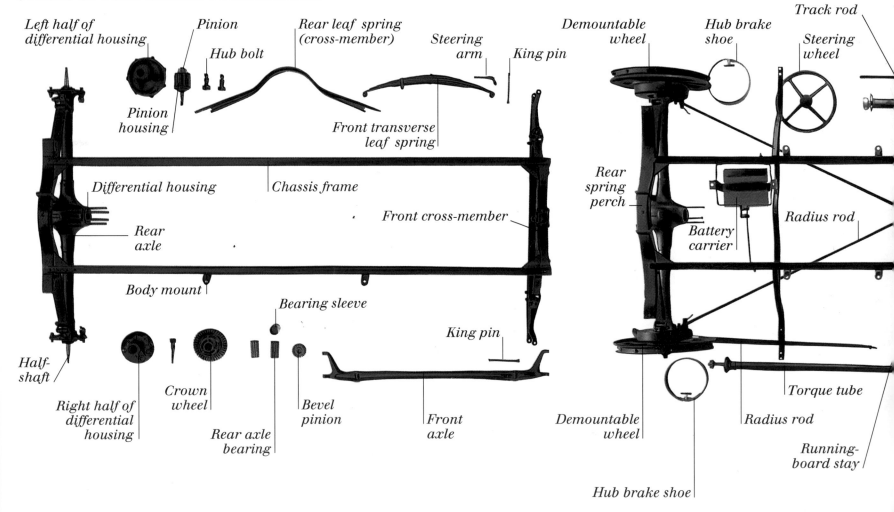

Left half of differential housing
Pinion
Rear leaf spring (cross-member)
Steering arm
King pin
Demountable wheel
Hub brake shoe
Track rod
Hub bolt
Steering wheel
Pinion housing
Front transverse leaf spring
Differential housing
Chassis frame
Rear spring perch
Rear axle
Front cross-member
Body mount
Bearing sleeve
Battery carrier
Radius rod
Half-shaft
King pin
Right half of differential housing
Crown wheel
Bevel pinion
Front axle
Demountable wheel
Radius rod
Torque tube
Rear axle bearing
Running-board stay
Hub brake shoe

SIDE VIEW OF 1913 FORD MODEL T

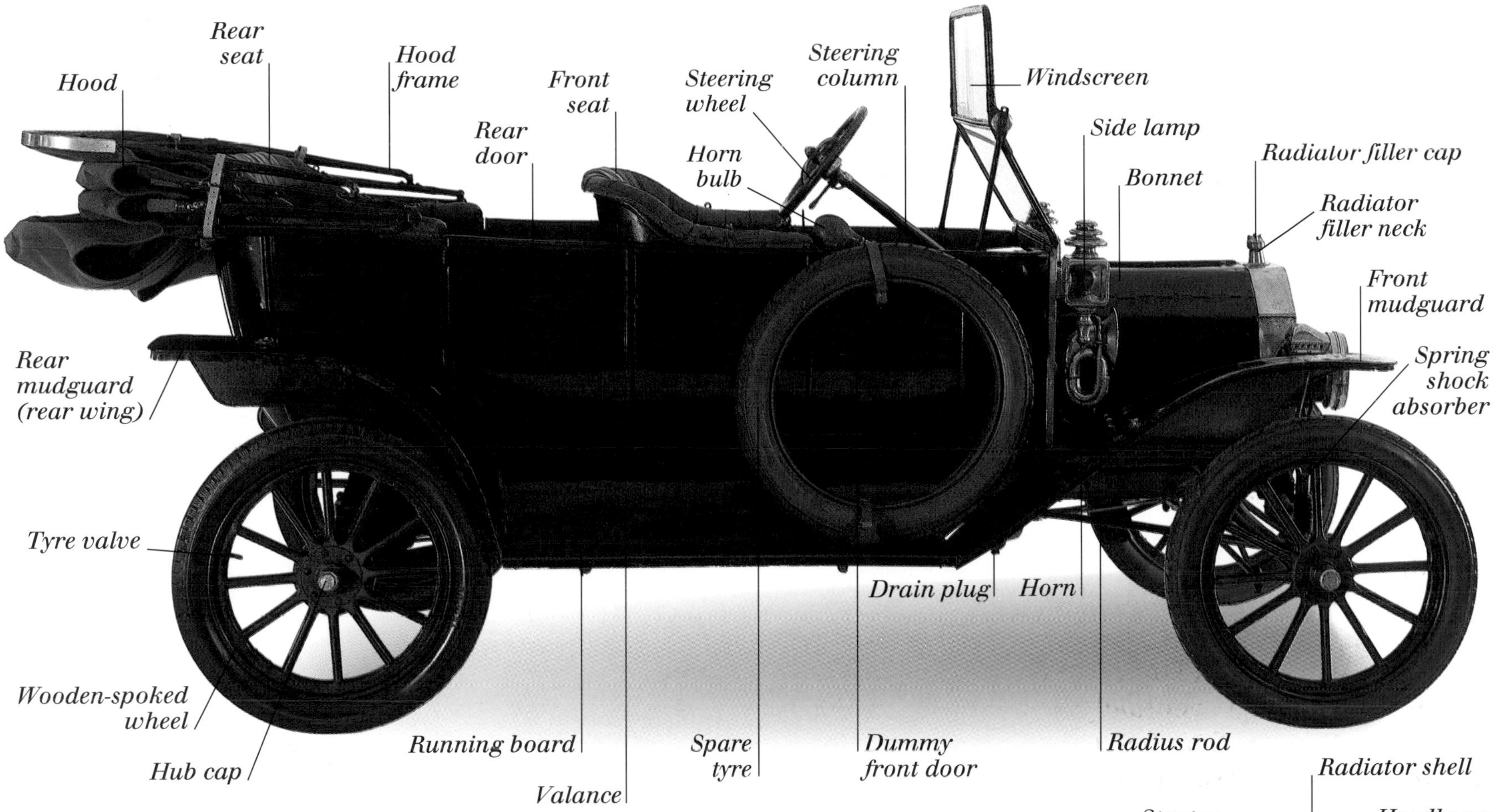

Hood

Rear seat

Hood frame

Front seat

Rear door

Steering wheel

Steering column

Horn bulb

Windscreen

Side lamp

Bonnet

Radiator filler cap

Radiator filler neck

Front mudguard

Spring shock absorber

Rear mudguard (rear wing)

Tyre valve

Wooden-spoked wheel

Hub cap

Running board

Valance

Spare tyre

Drain plug

Horn

Dummy front door

Radius rod

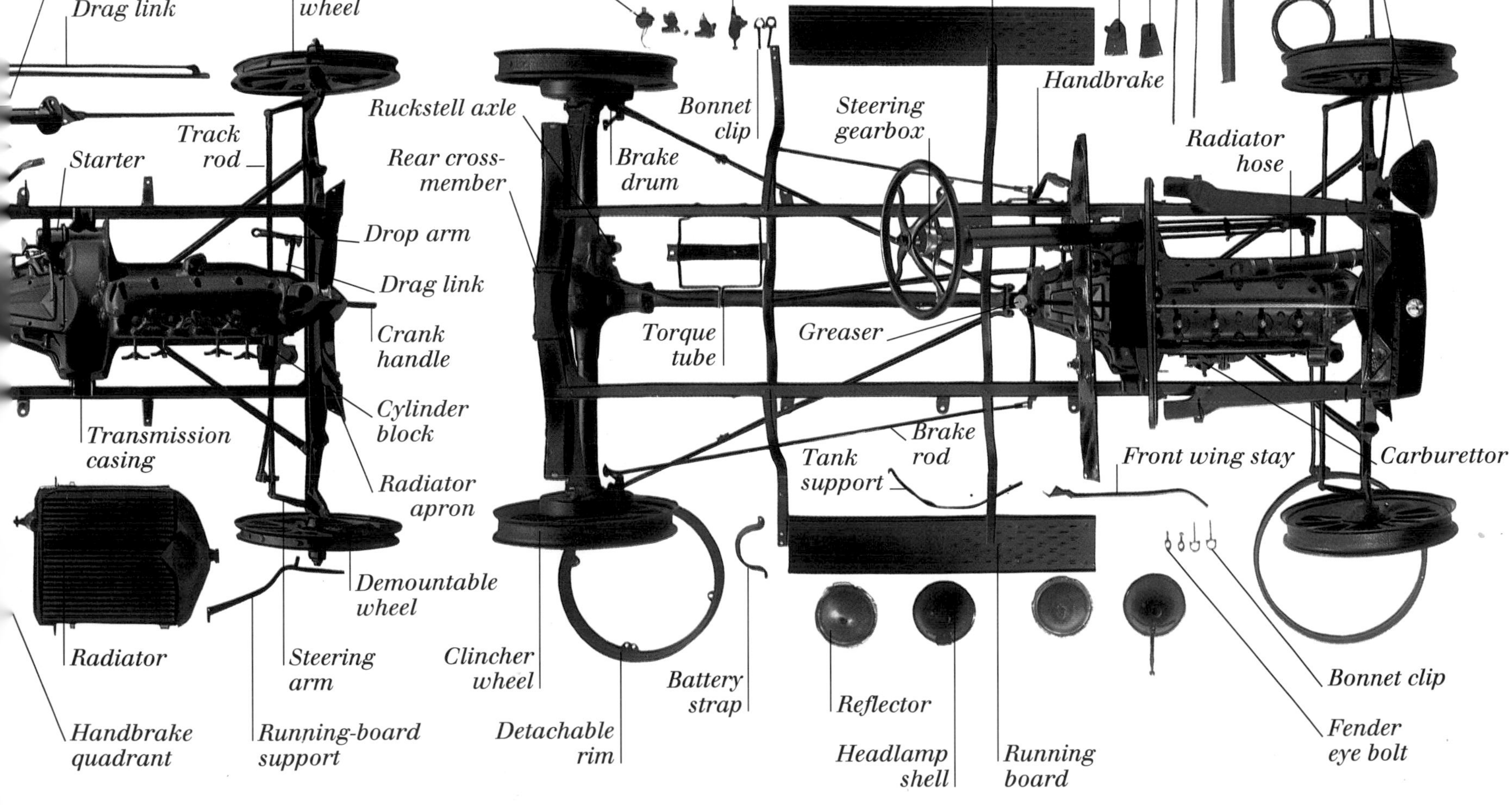

Radiator shell

Steering column

Drag link

Starter

Track rod

Transmission casing

Radiator

Handbrake quadrant

Demountable wheel

Ruckstell axle

Rear cross-member

Drop arm

Drag link

Crank handle

Cylinder block

Radiator apron

Demountable wheel

Steering arm

Running-board support

Bun lamp burner

Fuel sediment bowl

Bonnet clip

Brake drum

Torque tube

Tank support

Clincher wheel

Detachable rim

Battery strap

Running-board bracket

Steering gearbox

Greaser

Brake rod

Reflector

Headlamp shell

Light switch

Handbrake

Starter switch

Radiator hose

Front wing stay

Running board

Headlamp rim

Headlamp

Carburettor

Bonnet clip

Fender eye bolt

11

The "people's car"

THE MOST POPULAR CAR in the history of car manufacture is the Volkswagen Beetle, originally called the KdF Wagen. The car was developed in Germany in the 1930s by Dr. Ferdinand Porsche. At that time, Germany had only half the number of cars of Britain or France, and Adolf Hitler took a personal interest in the development of the Volkswagen ("people's car"). The intention was to provide a new industry, new jobs, and a car so cheap that anyone in work could afford it. Dr. Porsche designed a car that was cheap to build and run; its rear-mounted, air-cooled engine cut down the number of parts needed and also reduced weight. However, few civilians managed to obtain the Beetle before the outbreak of the Second World War in 1939. After the war, the Beetle proved so popular that eventually more than 20 million were sold.

CUSTOMIZED VOLKSWAGEN BEETLE

FLAT-FOUR CYLINDER ARRANGEMENT

WORKING PARTS OF VOLKSWAGEN BEETLE

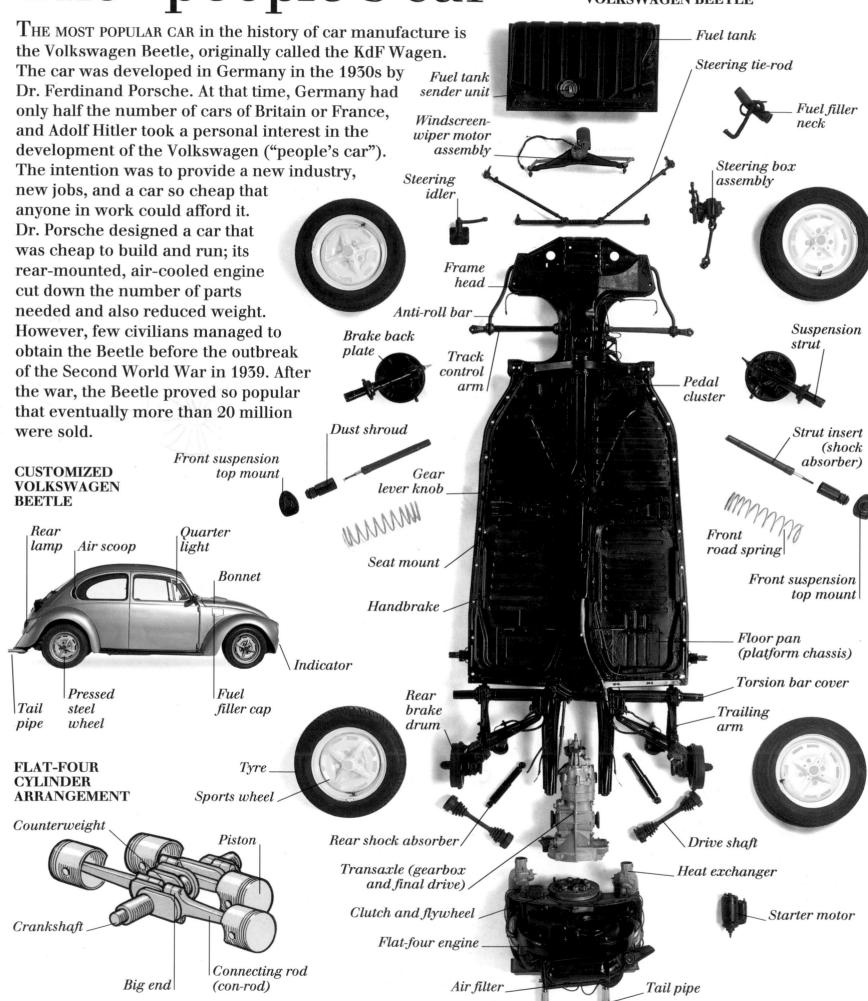

Fuel tank

Steering tie-rod

Fuel tank sender unit

Windscreen-wiper motor assembly

Fuel filler neck

Steering idler

Steering box assembly

Frame head

Anti-roll bar

Suspension strut

Brake back plate

Track control arm

Pedal cluster

Dust shroud

Strut insert (shock absorber)

Front suspension top mount

Gear lever knob

Seat mount

Front road spring

Handbrake

Front suspension top mount

Floor pan (platform chassis)

Torsion bar cover

Rear brake drum

Trailing arm

Tyre

Sports wheel

Rear shock absorber

Drive shaft

Transaxle (gearbox and final drive)

Heat exchanger

Clutch and flywheel

Flat-four engine

Starter motor

Air filter

Tail pipe

Rear lamp

Air scoop

Quarter light

Bonnet

Indicator

Tail pipe

Pressed steel wheel

Fuel filler cap

Counterweight

Piston

Crankshaft

Big end

Connecting rod (con-rod)

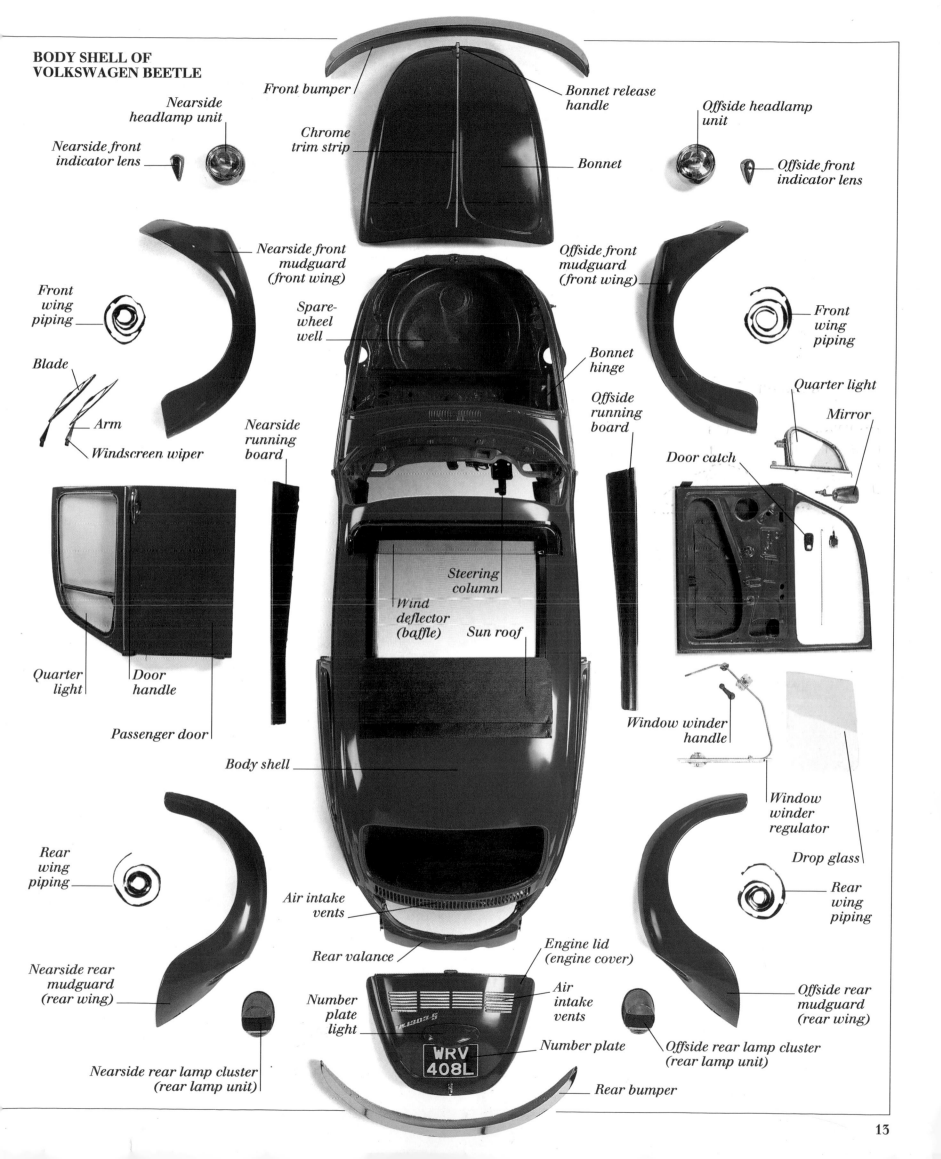

BODY SHELL OF VOLKSWAGEN BEETLE

Nearside headlamp unit

Nearside front indicator lens

Front bumper

Bonnet release handle

Chrome trim strip

Bonnet

Offside headlamp unit

Offside front indicator lens

Nearside front mudguard (front wing)

Front wing piping

Spare-wheel well

Bonnet hinge

Offside front mudguard (front wing)

Front wing piping

Blade

Arm

Windscreen wiper

Nearside running board

Offside running board

Quarter light

Mirror

Door catch

Quarter light

Door handle

Wind deflector (baffle)

Steering column

Sun roof

Passenger door

Window winder handle

Body shell

Window winder regulator

Rear wing piping

Drop glass

Air intake vents

Rear wing piping

Rear valance

Engine lid (engine cover)

Nearside rear mudguard (rear wing)

Number plate light

Air intake vents

Offside rear mudguard (rear wing)

Number plate

Offside rear lamp cluster (rear lamp unit)

Nearside rear lamp cluster (rear lamp unit)

WRV 408L

Rear bumper

Early engines

STEAM AND ELECTRICITY were used to power cars until early this century, but neither power source was ideal. Electric cars had to stop frequently to recharge their heavy batteries, and steam cars gave smooth power delivery but were too complicated for the average motorist to use. A rival power source, the internal combustion engine, was invented in 1860 by Etienne Lenoir (see pp. 6-7). This engine converted the force of an explosion into rotary motion, to turn the wheels of a vehicle. Early variations on this basic model included sleeve valves, separately cast cylinders, and the two-stroke combustion cycle. Today, all combustion engines, including the Wankel rotary and diesels (see pp. 18-19), use the four-stroke cycle, first demonstrated by Nikolaus Otto in 1876. The Otto cycle, often described as "suck, squeeze, bang, blow", has proved the best method of ensuring that the engine turns over smoothly and that exhaust emissions are controllable.

TROJAN TWO-STROKE ENGINE, 1927

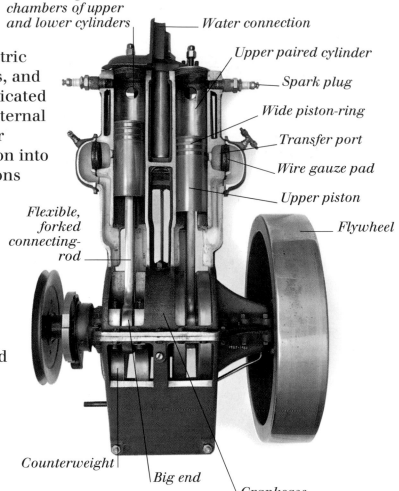

Port linking combustion chambers of upper and lower cylinders

Water connection

Upper paired cylinder

Spark plug

Wide piston-ring

Transfer port

Wire gauze pad

Upper piston

Flexible, forked connecting-rod

Flywheel

Counterweight

Big end

Crankcase

BERSEY ELECTRIC CAB, 1896

Mounting for tray of 40 batteries

Housing for electric motors

SECTIONED WHITE STEAM CAR, 1903

Steering wheel

Throttle wheel

Brake lever

Reverse lever

Automatic cylinder lubricator

Flash steam generator

Lamp bracket

High-pressure cylinder

Rocking lever

Exhaust pipe

Water pump

Condenser

Low-pressure cylinder

Fuel tank

Semi-elliptic spring

Brake drum

Spiral tubes

Flitch-plated wooden chassis

Drop arm

Water tank

Drag link

Dumb iron

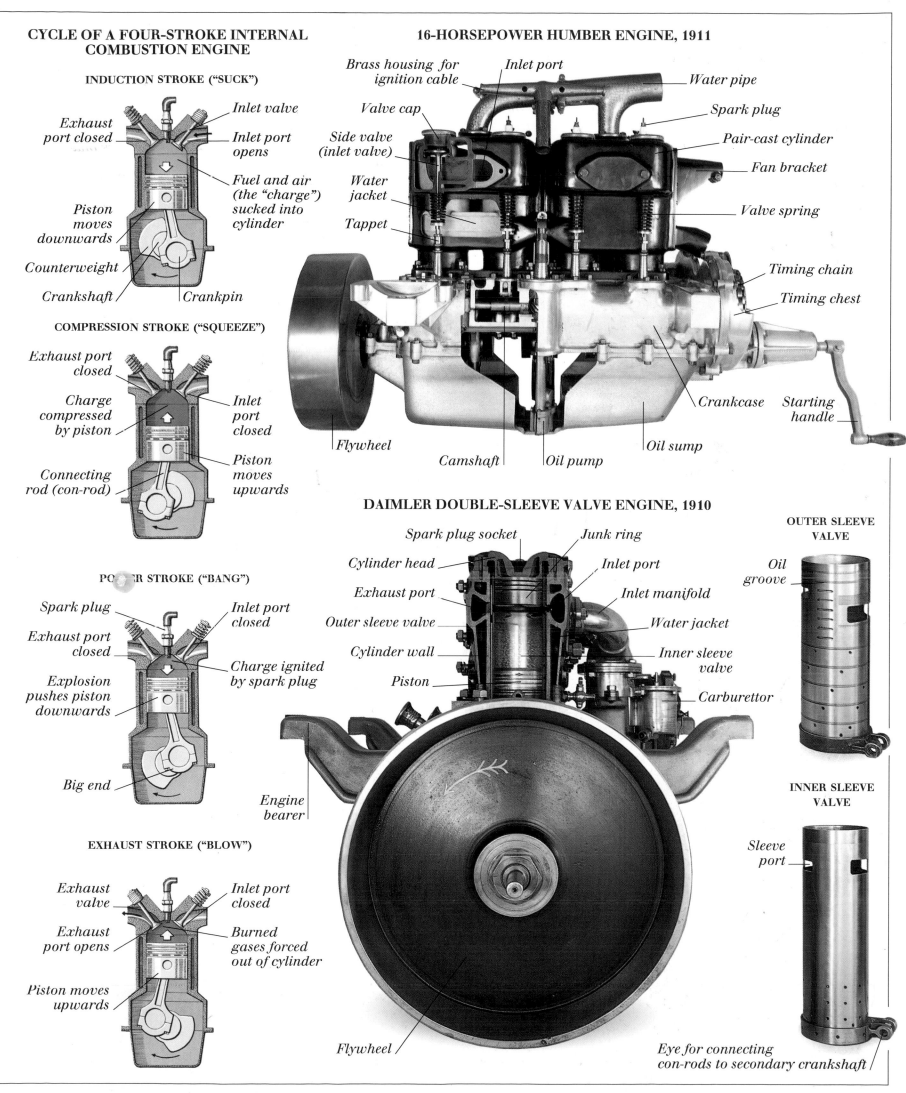

CYCLE OF A FOUR-STROKE INTERNAL COMBUSTION ENGINE

INDUCTION STROKE ("SUCK")

Exhaust port closed

Piston moves downwards

Counterweight

Crankshaft

Inlet valve

Inlet port opens

Fuel and air (the "charge") sucked into cylinder

Crankpin

COMPRESSION STROKE ("SQUEEZE")

Exhaust port closed

Charge compressed by piston

Connecting rod (con-rod)

Inlet port closed

Piston moves upwards

POWER STROKE ("BANG")

Spark plug

Exhaust port closed

Explosion pushes piston downwards

Big end

Inlet port closed

Charge ignited by spark plug

EXHAUST STROKE ("BLOW")

Exhaust valve

Exhaust port opens

Piston moves upwards

Inlet port closed

Burned gases forced out of cylinder

16-HORSEPOWER HUMBER ENGINE, 1911

Brass housing for ignition cable

Valve cap

Side valve (inlet valve)

Water jacket

Tappet

Inlet port

Water pipe

Spark plug

Pair-cast cylinder

Fan bracket

Valve spring

Timing chain

Timing chest

Flywheel

Camshaft

Oil pump

Crankcase

Oil sump

Starting handle

DAIMLER DOUBLE-SLEEVE VALVE ENGINE, 1910

Spark plug socket

Cylinder head

Exhaust port

Outer sleeve valve

Cylinder wall

Piston

Junk ring

Inlet port

Inlet manifold

Water jacket

Inner sleeve valve

Carburettor

Engine bearer

Flywheel

OUTER SLEEVE VALVE

Oil groove

INNER SLEEVE VALVE

Sleeve port

Eye for connecting con-rods to secondary crankshaft

Modern engines

TODAY'S PETROL ENGINE WORKS on the same basic principles as the first car engines of a century ago, although it has been greatly refined. Modern engines, often made from special metal alloys, are much lighter than earlier engines. Computerized ignition systems (see pp. 22-23), fuel injectors (see pp. 24-25), and multi-valve cylinder heads achieve a more efficient combustion of the fuel/air mixture (the charge) so that less fuel is wasted. As a result of this greater efficiency, the power and performance of a modern engine are increased, and the level of pollution in the exhaust gases is reduced. Exhaust pollution levels today are also lowered by the increasing use of special filters called catalytic converters, which absorb many exhaust pollutants. The need to produce ever more efficient engines means that it can take up to seven years to develop a new engine for a family car, at a cost of many millions of pounds.

FRONT VIEW OF A FORD COSWORTH V6 12-VALVE

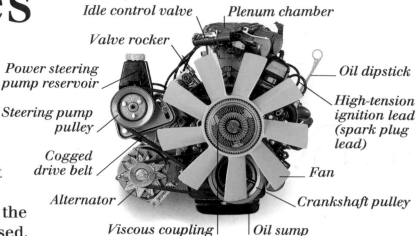

Idle control valve
Plenum chamber
Valve rocker
Power steering pump reservoir
Oil dipstick
Steering pump pulley
High-tension ignition lead (spark plug lead)
Cogged drive belt
Fan
Alternator
Crankshaft pulley
Viscous coupling
Oil sump

FRONT VIEW OF A FORD COSWORTH V6 24-VALVE

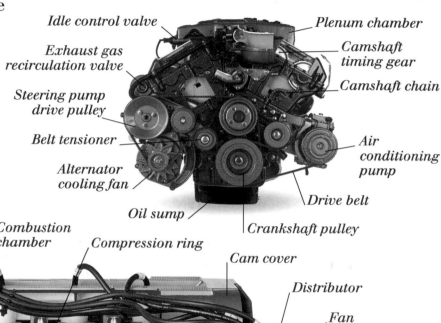

Idle control valve
Plenum chamber
Exhaust gas recirculation valve
Camshaft timing gear
Steering pump drive pulley
Camshaft chain
Belt tensioner
Air conditioning pump
Alternator cooling fan
Oil sump
Drive belt
Crankshaft pulley

SECTIONED VIEW OF A JAGUAR STRAIGHT 6

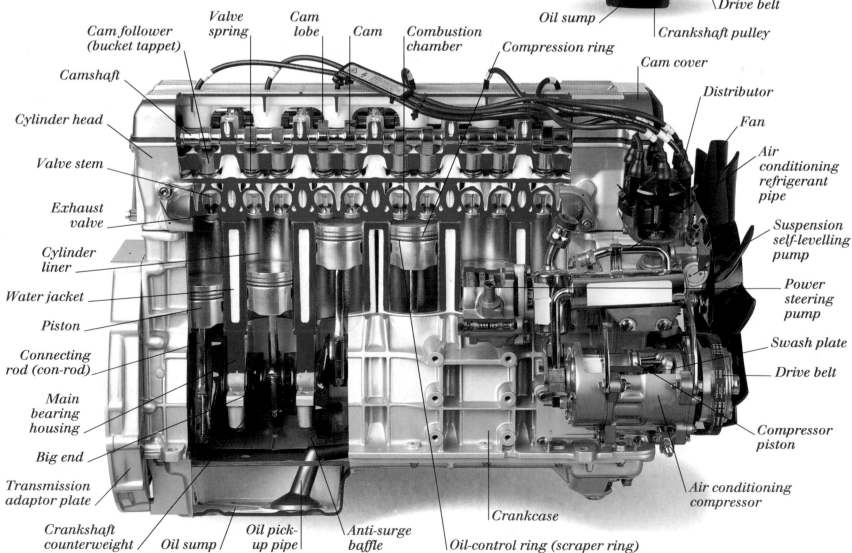

Cam follower (bucket tappet)
Valve spring
Cam lobe
Cam
Combustion chamber
Compression ring
Camshaft
Cam cover
Cylinder head
Distributor
Valve stem
Fan
Exhaust valve
Air conditioning refrigerant pipe
Cylinder liner
Suspension self-levelling pump
Water jacket
Power steering pump
Piston
Swash plate
Connecting rod (con-rod)
Drive belt
Main bearing housing
Big end
Compressor piston
Transmission adaptor plate
Air conditioning compressor
Crankshaft counterweight
Oil sump
Oil pick-up pipe
Anti-surge baffle
Crankcase
Oil-control ring (scraper ring)

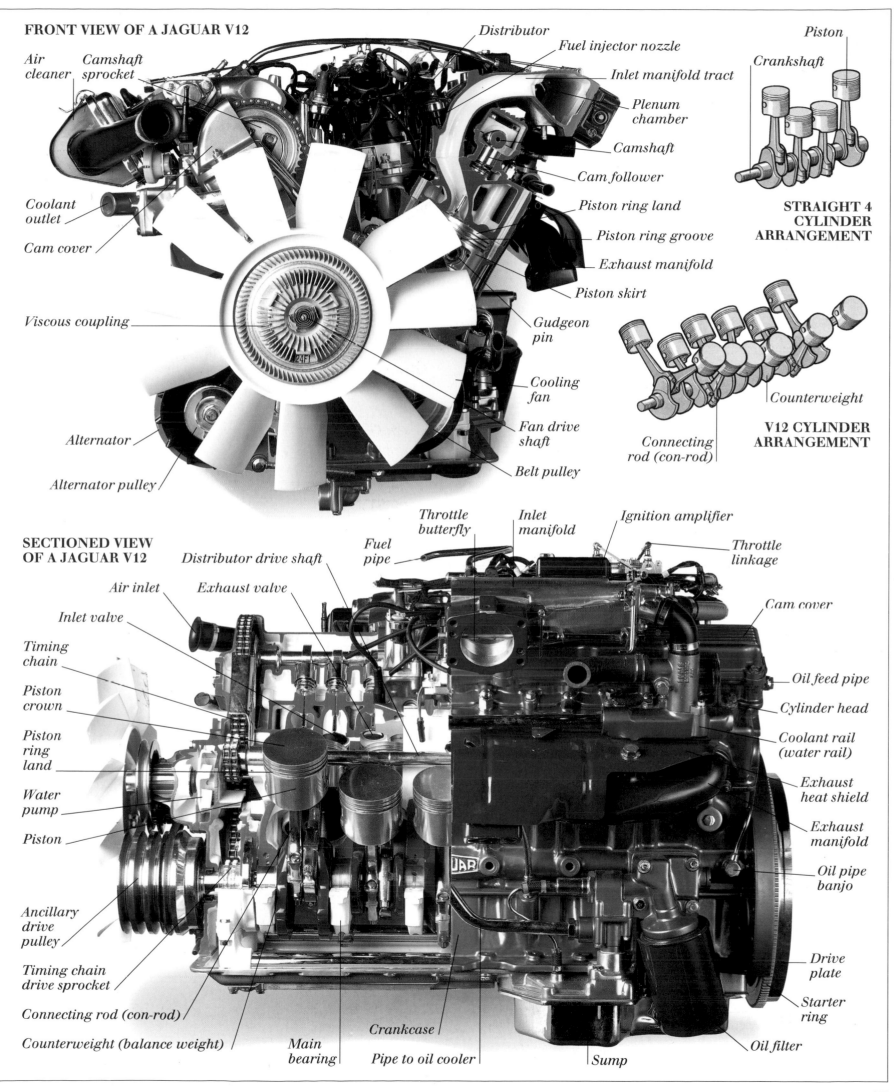

FRONT VIEW OF A JAGUAR V12

Air cleaner

Camshaft sprocket

Distributor

Fuel injector nozzle

Piston

Crankshaft

Inlet manifold tract

Plenum chamber

Camshaft

Cam follower

Piston ring land

Piston ring groove

Exhaust manifold

Piston skirt

STRAIGHT 4 CYLINDER ARRANGEMENT

Coolant outlet

Cam cover

Viscous coupling

Gudgeon pin

Cooling fan

Fan drive shaft

Counterweight

V12 CYLINDER ARRANGEMENT

Alternator

Alternator pulley

Belt pulley

Connecting rod (con-rod)

SECTIONED VIEW OF A JAGUAR V12

Throttle butterfly

Inlet manifold

Ignition amplifier

Throttle linkage

Fuel pipe

Distributor drive shaft

Air inlet

Exhaust valve

Inlet valve

Cam cover

Timing chain

Oil feed pipe

Piston crown

Cylinder head

Piston ring land

Coolant rail (water rail)

Water pump

Exhaust heat shield

Piston

Exhaust manifold

Oil pipe banjo

Ancillary drive pulley

Timing chain drive sprocket

Drive plate

Connecting rod (con-rod)

Starter ring

Counterweight (balance weight)

Main bearing

Crankcase

Pipe to oil cooler

Sump

Oil filter

17

Alternative engines

THE MOST COMMON TYPE OF ALTERNATIVE ENGINE is the diesel engine, which, instead of igniting the compressed fuel/air mixture with a spark, uses compression alone, heating the mixture to the point where it explodes. A diesel engine's fuel consumption is low in comparison with similarly sized piston engines, despite its heavier, reinforced moving parts and cylinder block. Another type of engine is the rotary-combustion, first successfully developed by Felix Wankel in the 1950s. Its two trilobate (three-sided) rotors revolve in housings shaped in a fat figure-of-eight. The four sequences of the four-stroke cycle, which occur consecutively in a piston engine, occur simultaneously in a rotary engine, producing power in a continuous stream.

ROTARY-ENGINED MAZDA RX-7

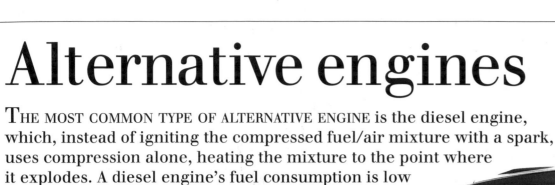

Aerodynamic windscreen

Headrest

Hood bag

Front spoiler (chin spoiler)

Side marker lamp

Rubbing strake

Cast alloy wheel

WANKEL ROTARY ENGINE

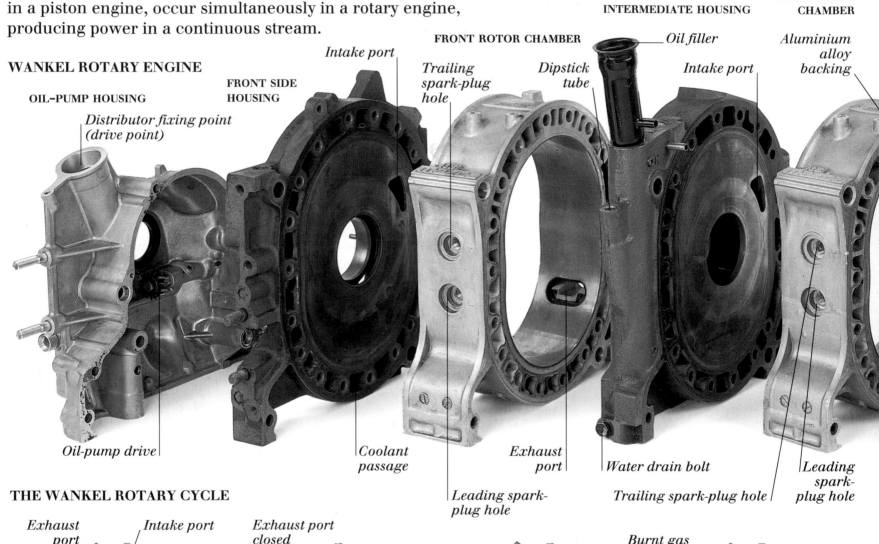

OIL-PUMP HOUSING

Distributor fixing point (drive point)

FRONT SIDE HOUSING

Intake port

FRONT ROTOR CHAMBER

Trailing spark-plug hole

Dipstick tube

Oil filler

INTERMEDIATE HOUSING

Intake port

REAR ROTOR CHAMBER

Aluminium alloy backing

Oil-pump drive

Coolant passage

Exhaust port

Leading spark-plug hole

Water drain bolt

Trailing spark-plug hole

Leading spark-plug hole

THE WANKEL ROTARY CYCLE

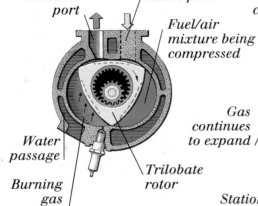

Exhaust port

Intake port

Fuel/air mixture being compressed

Water passage

Burning gas expands

Trilobate rotor

Exhaust port closed

Vacuum sucks in fuel/air mixture

Gas continues to expand

Stationary gear (fixed gear)

Compression continues

Burnt gas exhausts

Rotor gear

Compressed gas ignites

Fuel/air mixture continues to enter

Burnt gas continues to exhaust

Output shaft turns

Burnt gas begins to expand

Compression begins

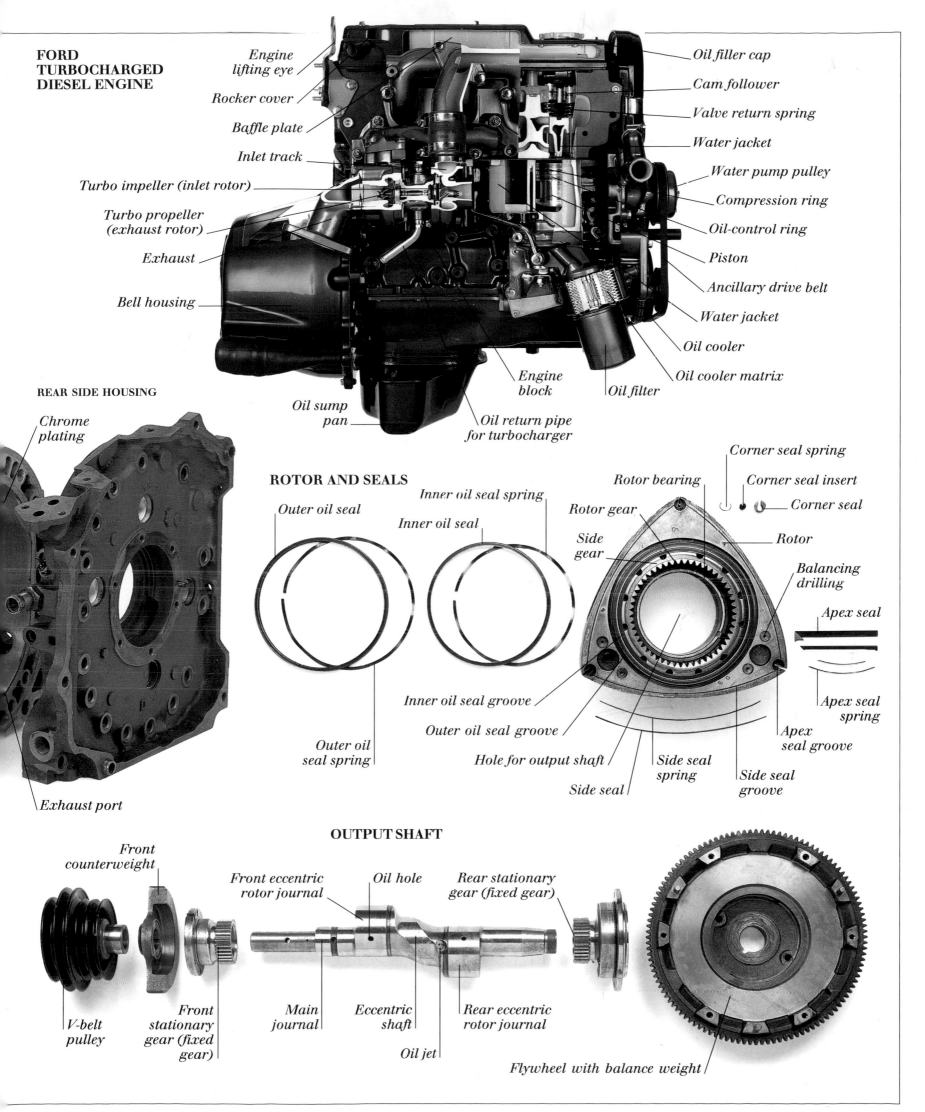

FORD TURBOCHARGED DIESEL ENGINE

Engine lifting eye

Rocker cover

Baffle plate

Inlet track

Turbo impeller (inlet rotor)

Turbo propeller (exhaust rotor)

Exhaust

Bell housing

Oil filler cap

Cam follower

Valve return spring

Water jacket

Water pump pulley

Compression ring

Oil-control ring

Piston

Ancillary drive belt

Water jacket

Oil cooler

Oil cooler matrix

Oil filter

Engine block

Oil sump pan

Oil return pipe for turbocharger

REAR SIDE HOUSING

Chrome plating

Exhaust port

ROTOR AND SEALS

Outer oil seal

Inner oil seal spring

Inner oil seal

Corner seal spring

Corner seal insert

Corner seal

Rotor bearing

Rotor gear

Side gear

Rotor

Balancing drilling

Apex seal

Outer oil seal spring

Inner oil seal groove

Outer oil seal groove

Hole for output shaft

Side seal spring

Side seal

Side seal groove

Apex seal groove

Apex seal spring

OUTPUT SHAFT

Front counterweight

Front eccentric rotor journal

Oil hole

Rear stationary gear (fixed gear)

V-belt pulley

Front stationary gear (fixed gear)

Main journal

Eccentric shaft

Oil jet

Rear eccentric rotor journal

Flywheel with balance weight

Carburettors

CARBURETTORS MIX FUEL VAPOUR AND AIR to create a gas (the "charge") that will explode when compressed and ignited in the engine cylinders. The fuel and air must be mixed in exactly the right proportions, which vary with speed and load, for the engine to work with maximum efficiency. The amount of air entering the carburettor is altered by opening and closing the throttle using the accelerator pedal. The air flows quickly as it enters a narrow passage called the venturi. Here, the air passes over a narrow jet linked to a small petrol reservoir (the float chamber) and causes fuel to be sucked from the jet in a fine mist. To control the amount of fuel and air some carburettors vary the size of the venturi, others the size of the fuel jets. Today, fuel injectors are increasingly replacing carburettors.

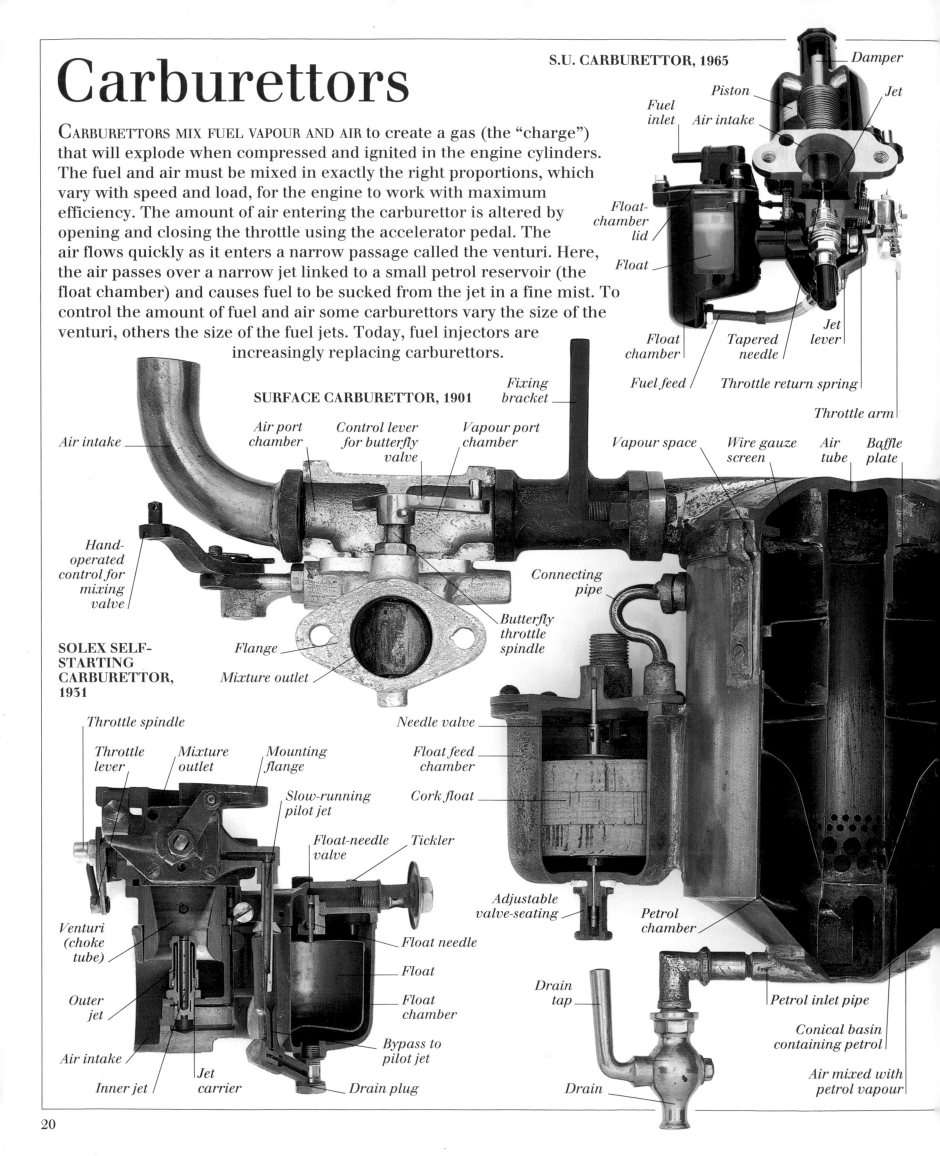

S.U. CARBURETTOR, 1965

Damper · Piston · Jet · Fuel inlet · Air intake · Float-chamber lid · Float · Float chamber · Tapered needle · Fuel feed · Jet lever · Throttle return spring · Throttle arm

SURFACE CARBURETTOR, 1901

Fixing bracket · Air intake · Air port chamber · Control lever for butterfly valve · Vapour port chamber · Vapour space · Wire gauze screen · Air tube · Baffle plate · Hand-operated control for mixing valve · Connecting pipe · Butterfly throttle spindle · Flange · Mixture outlet

SOLEX SELF-STARTING CARBURETTOR, 1931

Throttle spindle · Throttle lever · Mixture outlet · Mounting flange · Slow-running pilot jet · Float-needle valve · Tickler · Venturi (choke tube) · Outer jet · Air intake · Inner jet · Jet carrier · Drain plug · Float needle · Float · Float chamber · Bypass to pilot jet · Needle valve · Float feed chamber · Cork float · Adjustable valve-seating · Petrol chamber · Drain tap · Drain · Petrol inlet pipe · Conical basin containing petrol · Air mixed with petrol vapour

20

WEBER TWIN VENTURI CARBURETTOR, 1991

WEBER TWIN VENTURI CARBURETTOR, 1991

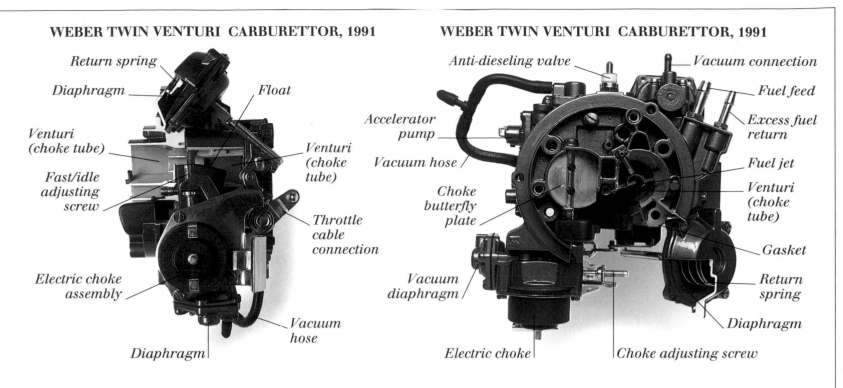

Return spring

Diaphragm

Float

Venturi (choke tube)

Venturi (choke tube)

Fast/idle adjusting screw

Throttle cable connection

Electric choke assembly

Vacuum hose

Diaphragm

Anti-dieseling valve

Vacuum connection

Accelerator pump

Fuel feed

Excess fuel return

Vacuum hose

Fuel jet

Choke butterfly plate

Venturi (choke tube)

Gasket

Vacuum diaphragm

Return spring

Diaphragm

Electric choke

Choke adjusting screw

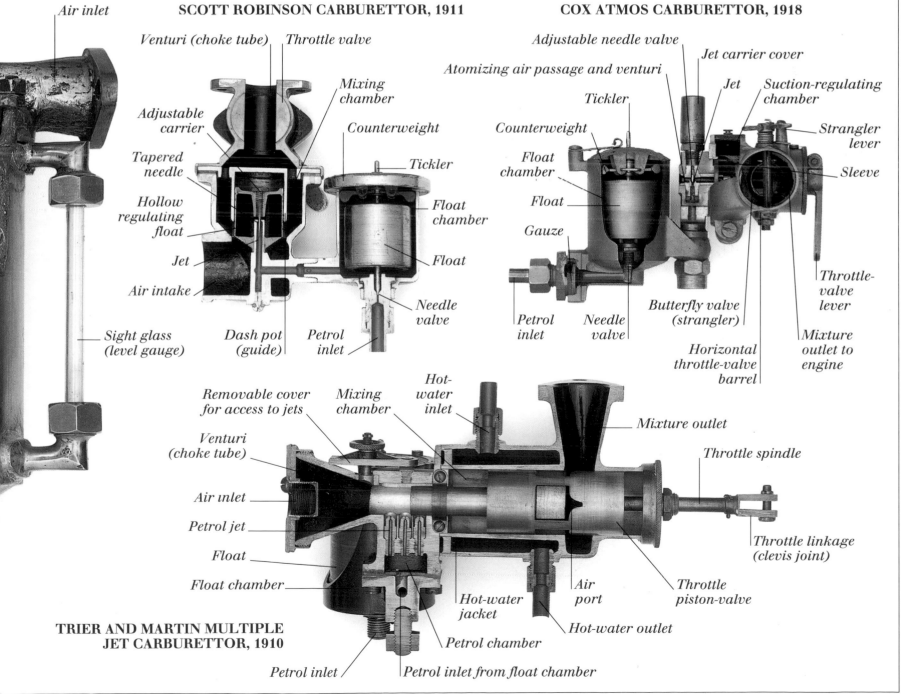

SCOTT ROBINSON CARBURETTOR, 1911

Air inlet

Venturi (choke tube)

Throttle valve

Mixing chamber

Adjustable carrier

Counterweight

Tapered needle

Tickler

Hollow regulating float

Float chamber

Jet

Float

Air intake

Sight glass (level gauge)

Dash pot (guide)

Petrol inlet

Needle valve

COX ATMOS CARBURETTOR, 1918

Adjustable needle valve

Jet carrier cover

Atomizing air passage and venturi

Jet

Tickler

Suction-regulating chamber

Counterweight

Strangler lever

Float chamber

Sleeve

Float

Gauze

Petrol inlet

Needle valve

Butterfly valve (strangler)

Horizontal throttle-valve barrel

Throttle-valve lever

Mixture outlet to engine

TRIER AND MARTIN MULTIPLE JET CARBURETTOR, 1910

Removable cover for access to jets

Mixing chamber

Hot-water inlet

Venturi (choke tube)

Mixture outlet

Air inlet

Throttle spindle

Petrol jet

Float

Throttle linkage (clevis joint)

Float chamber

Air port

Throttle piston-valve

Hot-water jacket

Petrol inlet

Hot-water outlet

Petrol chamber

Petrol inlet from float chamber

Ignition systems

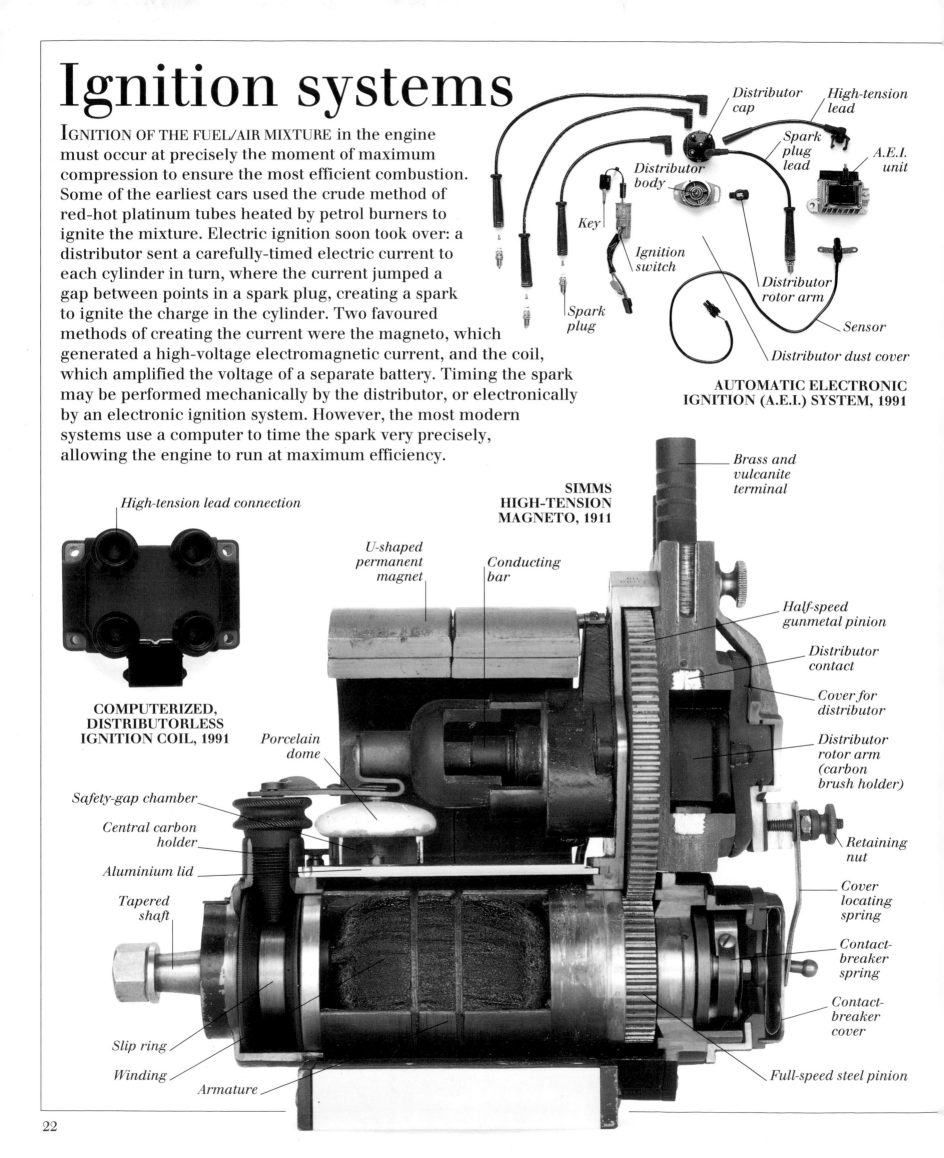

IGNITION OF THE FUEL/AIR MIXTURE in the engine must occur at precisely the moment of maximum compression to ensure the most efficient combustion. Some of the earliest cars used the crude method of red-hot platinum tubes heated by petrol burners to ignite the mixture. Electric ignition soon took over: a distributor sent a carefully-timed electric current to each cylinder in turn, where the current jumped a gap between points in a spark plug, creating a spark to ignite the charge in the cylinder. Two favoured methods of creating the current were the magneto, which generated a high-voltage electromagnetic current, and the coil, which amplified the voltage of a separate battery. Timing the spark may be performed mechanically by the distributor, or electronically by an electronic ignition system. However, the most modern systems use a computer to time the spark very precisely, allowing the engine to run at maximum efficiency.

AUTOMATIC ELECTRONIC IGNITION (A.E.I.) SYSTEM, 1991

Distributor cap

High-tension lead

Spark plug lead

A.E.I. unit

Distributor body

Key

Ignition switch

Spark plug

Distributor rotor arm

Sensor

Distributor dust cover

SIMMS HIGH-TENSION MAGNETO, 1911

Brass and vulcanite terminal

U-shaped permanent magnet

Conducting bar

Half-speed gunmetal pinion

Distributor contact

Cover for distributor

Distributor rotor arm (carbon brush holder)

Retaining nut

Cover locating spring

Contact-breaker spring

Contact-breaker cover

Full-speed steel pinion

High-tension lead connection

COMPUTERIZED, DISTRIBUTORLESS IGNITION COIL, 1991

Porcelain dome

Safety-gap chamber

Central carbon holder

Aluminium lid

Tapered shaft

Slip ring

Winding

Armature

LODGE LOW-TENSION IGNITION COIL, 1907

PEUGEOT WITH HOT-TUBE IGNITION, 1896

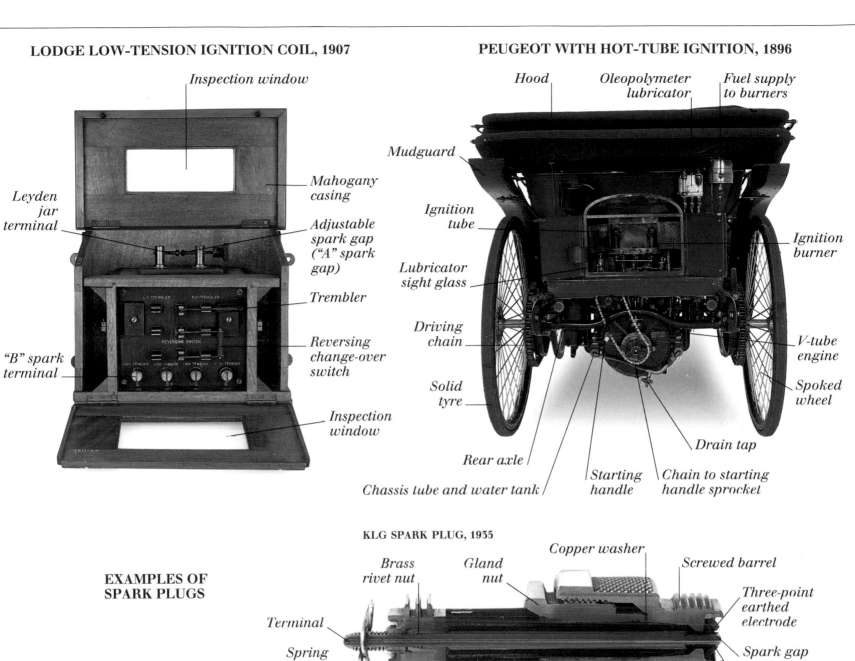

Inspection window

Leyden jar terminal

Mahogany casing

Adjustable spark gap ("A" spark gap)

Trembler

"B" spark terminal

Reversing change-over switch

Inspection window

Hood

Oleopolymeter lubricator

Fuel supply to burners

Mudguard

Ignition tube

Lubricator sight glass

Driving chain

Solid tyre

Ignition burner

V-tube engine

Spoked wheel

Drain tap

Rear axle

Starting handle

Chain to starting handle sprocket

Chassis tube and water tank

KLG SPARK PLUG, 1935

EXAMPLES OF SPARK PLUGS

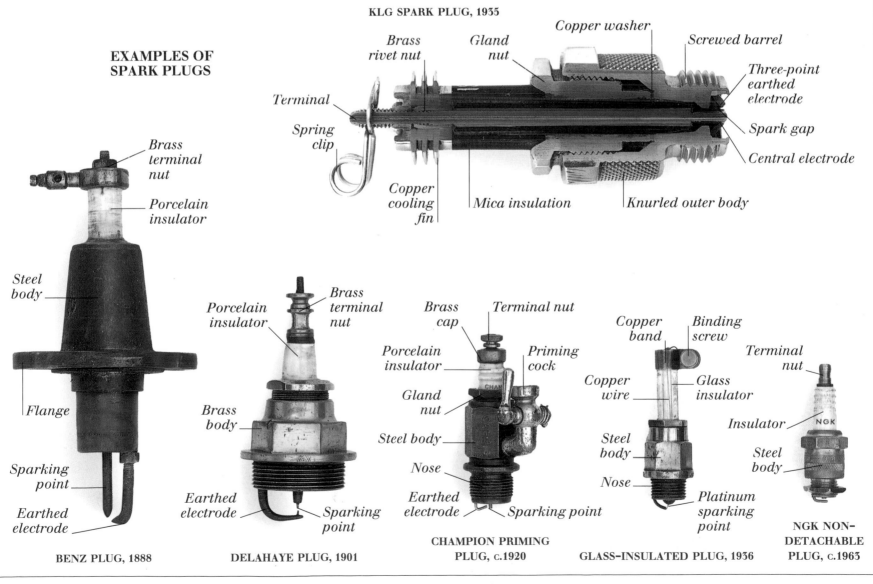

Brass rivet nut

Gland nut

Copper washer

Screwed barrel

Terminal

Spring clip

Three-point earthed electrode

Spark gap

Central electrode

Copper cooling fin

Mica insulation

Knurled outer body

Brass terminal nut

Porcelain insulator

Steel body

Flange

Sparking point

Earthed electrode

BENZ PLUG, 1888

Porcelain insulator

Brass terminal nut

Brass body

Earthed electrode

Sparking point

DELAHAYE PLUG, 1901

Brass cap

Terminal nut

Porcelain insulator

Priming cock

Gland nut

Steel body

Nose

Earthed electrode

Sparking point

CHAMPION PRIMING PLUG, c.1920

Copper band

Binding screw

Copper wire

Glass insulator

Steel body

Nose

Platinum sparking point

GLASS-INSULATED PLUG, 1936

Terminal nut

Insulator

Steel body

NGK NON-DETACHABLE PLUG, c.1963

Power-boosters

AN ENGINE'S POWER OUTPUT can be increased by forcing more of the fuel/air mixture (the charge) into the cylinders (forced induction) to provide a bigger explosion on the power stroke. There are two types of forced induction: supercharging and turbocharging. A supercharger, or blower, uses rotating vanes or lobes to force air into the engine; the increased flow of air sucks (or blows) more fuel vapour in, increasing the charge in the cylinders. Superchargers are driven by the engine, using some of its power. Turbochargers do the same job but are driven by exhaust gases and so do not use any of the engine's power. The power and efficiency of an engine can also be increased by fuel injectors, which have regulators that react to the engine's requirements by injecting exactly the right amount of fuel.

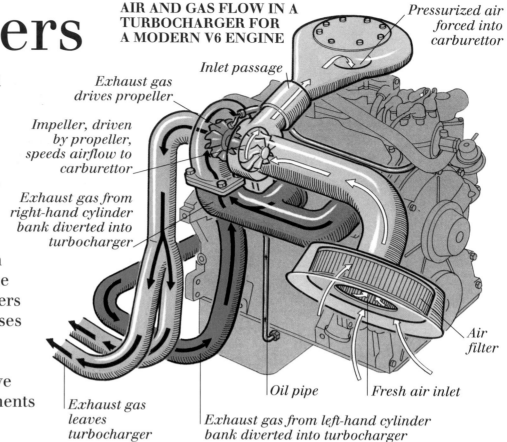

AIR AND GAS FLOW IN A TURBOCHARGER FOR A MODERN V6 ENGINE

Pressurized air forced into carburettor

Inlet passage

Exhaust gas drives propeller

Impeller, driven by propeller, speeds airflow to carburettor

Exhaust gas from right-hand cylinder bank diverted into turbocharger

Air filter

Oil pipe

Fresh air inlet

Exhaust gas leaves turbocharger

Exhaust gas from left-hand cylinder bank diverted into turbocharger

PARTS OF A SUPERCHARGER, c.1948

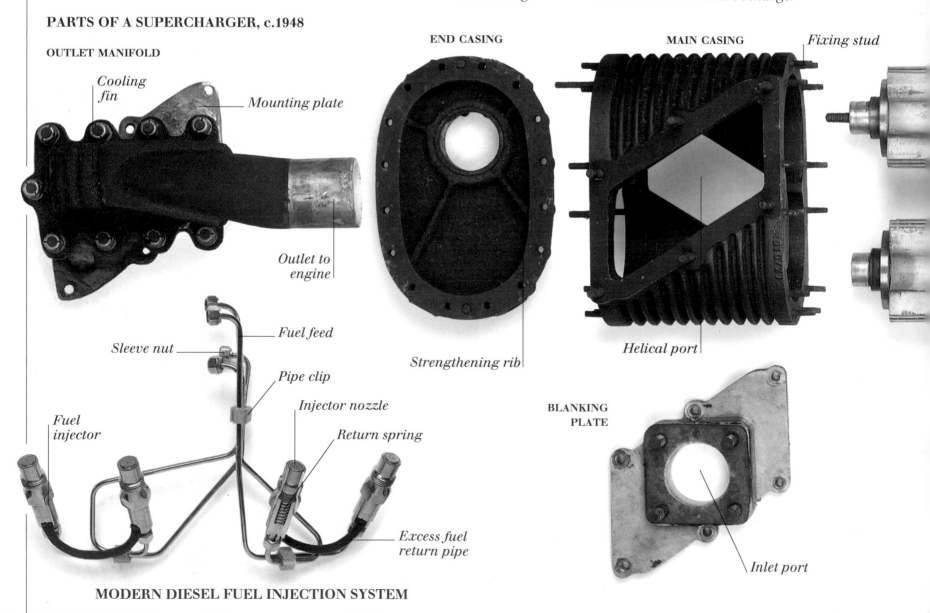

OUTLET MANIFOLD

Cooling fin

Mounting plate

Outlet to engine

END CASING

MAIN CASING

Fixing stud

Strengthening rib

Helical port

Fuel feed

Sleeve nut

Pipe clip

Injector nozzle

Return spring

Fuel injector

Excess fuel return pipe

BLANKING PLATE

Inlet port

MODERN DIESEL FUEL INJECTION SYSTEM

24

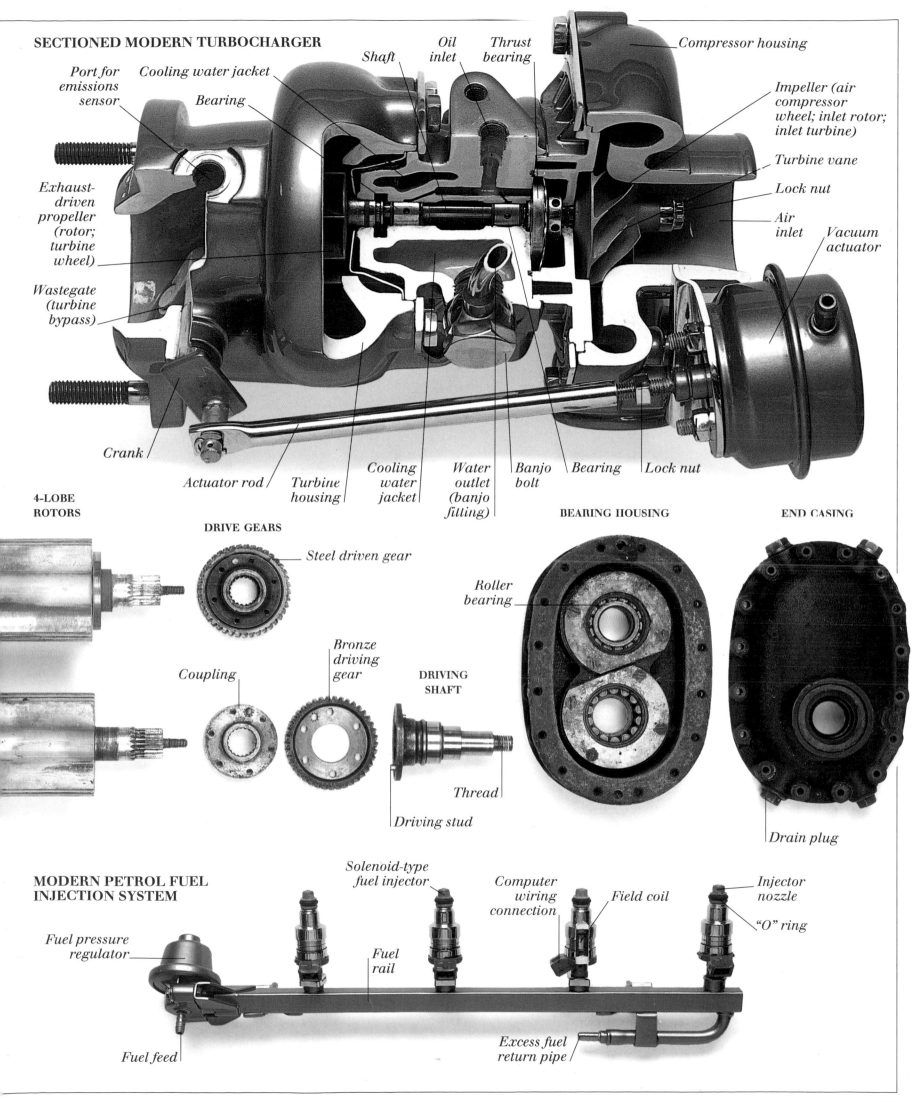

SECTIONED MODERN TURBOCHARGER

Port for emissions sensor

Cooling water jacket

Bearing

Shaft

Oil inlet

Thrust bearing

Compressor housing

Impeller (air compressor wheel; inlet rotor; inlet turbine)

Turbine vane

Lock nut

Air inlet

Vacuum actuator

Exhaust-driven propeller (rotor; turbine wheel)

Wastegate (turbine bypass)

Crank

Actuator rod

Turbine housing

Cooling water jacket

Water outlet (banjo filling)

Banjo bolt

Bearing

Lock nut

4-LOBE ROTORS

DRIVE GEARS

Steel driven gear

Coupling

Bronze driving gear

Roller bearing

BEARING HOUSING

END CASING

DRIVING SHAFT

Thread

Driving stud

Drain plug

MODERN PETROL FUEL INJECTION SYSTEM

Solenoid-type fuel injector

Computer wiring connection

Field coil

Injector nozzle

"O" ring

Fuel pressure regulator

Fuel rail

Fuel feed

Excess fuel return pipe

Cooling and lubrication

COMBUSTION TEMPERATURES in an engine's cylinders can reach around 1,700°C (3,000°F), enough heat to melt the cylinder head. To prevent this, most cars have a water-cooling system, although a few cars use air-cooling. Coolant (water mixed with antifreeze) is circulated around a jacket surrounding the cylinders, then to a radiator, where the heat the coolant has absorbed is released into the air. Some heat may be used to warm the car's interior. Modern vehicles increasingly use separate air-conditioning systems to maintain a steady temperature. Oil lubrication also cools the engine, but its main role is to maintain a thin film of oil between moving parts to prevent wearing and seizing. Most lubrication systems circulate oil from a sump attached to the engine. The dry sump lubrication system, used in some competition cars, keeps oil in a tank separate from the engine, to prevent the oil from overheating.

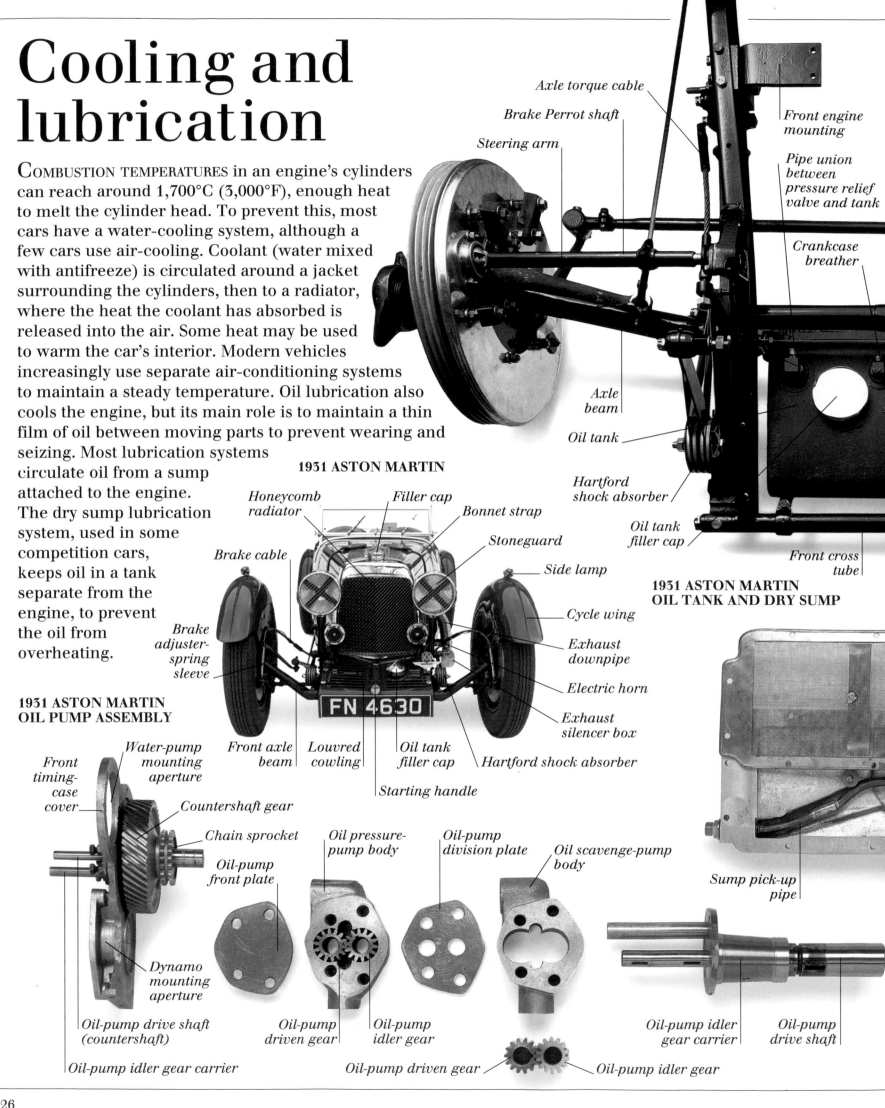

Axle torque cable

Brake Perrot shaft

Steering arm

Front engine mounting

Pipe union between pressure relief valve and tank

Crankcase breather

Axle beam

Oil tank

Hartford shock absorber

Oil tank filler cap

Front cross tube

1931 ASTON MARTIN OIL TANK AND DRY SUMP

1931 ASTON MARTIN

Honeycomb radiator

Filler cap

Bonnet strap

Brake cable

Stoneguard

Side lamp

Cycle wing

Brake adjuster-spring sleeve

Exhaust downpipe

Electric horn

Exhaust silencer box

Front axle beam

Louvred cowling

Oil tank filler cap

Hartford shock absorber

Starting handle

FN 4630

1931 ASTON MARTIN OIL PUMP ASSEMBLY

Front timing-case cover

Water-pump mounting aperture

Countershaft gear

Chain sprocket

Oil pressure-pump body

Oil-pump division plate

Oil scavenge-pump body

Oil-pump front plate

Sump pick-up pipe

Dynamo mounting aperture

Oil-pump drive shaft (countershaft)

Oil-pump driven gear

Oil-pump idler gear

Oil-pump idler gear carrier

Oil-pump drive shaft

Oil-pump idler gear carrier

Oil-pump driven gear

Oil-pump idler gear

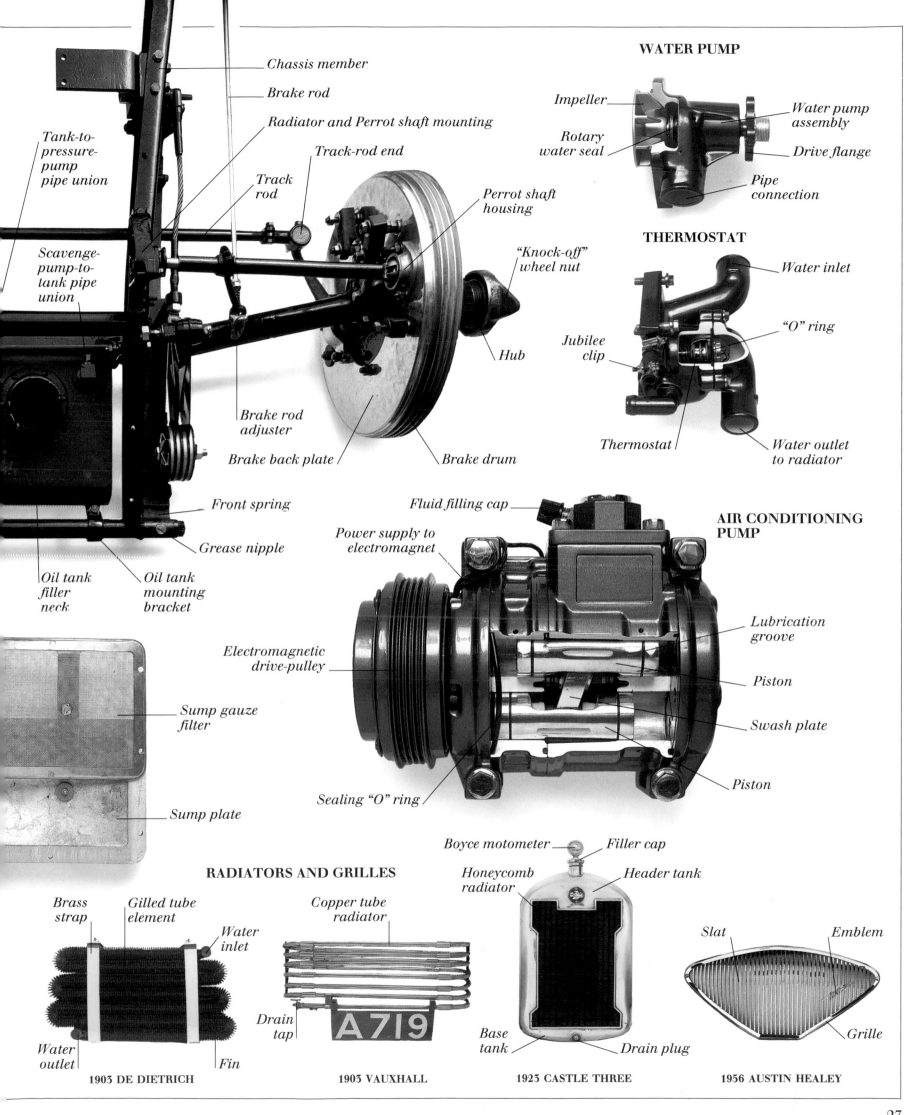

Chassis member

Brake rod

Radiator and Perrot shaft mounting

Track-rod end

Tank-to-pressure-pump pipe union

Track rod

Perrot shaft housing

Scavenge-pump-to-tank pipe union

"Knock-off" wheel nut

Hub

Brake rod adjuster

Brake back plate

Brake drum

Front spring

Grease nipple

Oil tank filler neck

Oil tank mounting bracket

Sump gauze filter

Sump plate

WATER PUMP

Impeller

Water pump assembly

Rotary water seal

Drive flange

Pipe connection

THERMOSTAT

Water inlet

"O" ring

Jubilee clip

Thermostat

Water outlet to radiator

AIR CONDITIONING PUMP

Fluid filling cap

Power supply to electromagnet

Electromagnetic drive-pulley

Lubrication groove

Piston

Swash plate

Sealing "O" ring

Piston

RADIATORS AND GRILLES

Boyce motometer

Filler cap

Honeycomb radiator

Header tank

Brass strap

Gilled tube element

Copper tube radiator

Water inlet

Slat

Emblem

Drain tap

A719

Grille

Water outlet

Fin

Base tank

Drain plug

1903 DE DIETRICH

1903 VAUXHALL

1923 CASTLE THREE

1956 AUSTIN HEALEY

27

Clutch and gearbox

THE GEARBOX TRANSMITS POWER from the engine to the road wheels, and also allows the wheels to turn at different speeds to the engine. Modern gearboxes contain five or six sets of intermeshed cogs (including a reverse gear set) to apply the turning force of the engine (torque) most efficiently over as wide a range of road speeds as possible and to enable the car to climb hills. To engage gears, or to remain stationary with the engine running, the engine must be disconnected from the gearbox. This is achieved by the clutch, which has one plate connected to the engine (the driving plate) and another connected to the gearbox (the driven plate). To disconnect the engine from the gearbox, the clutch plates are unclamped so that they are no longer in contact; for the engine to drive the wheels, strong springs clamp the plates together.

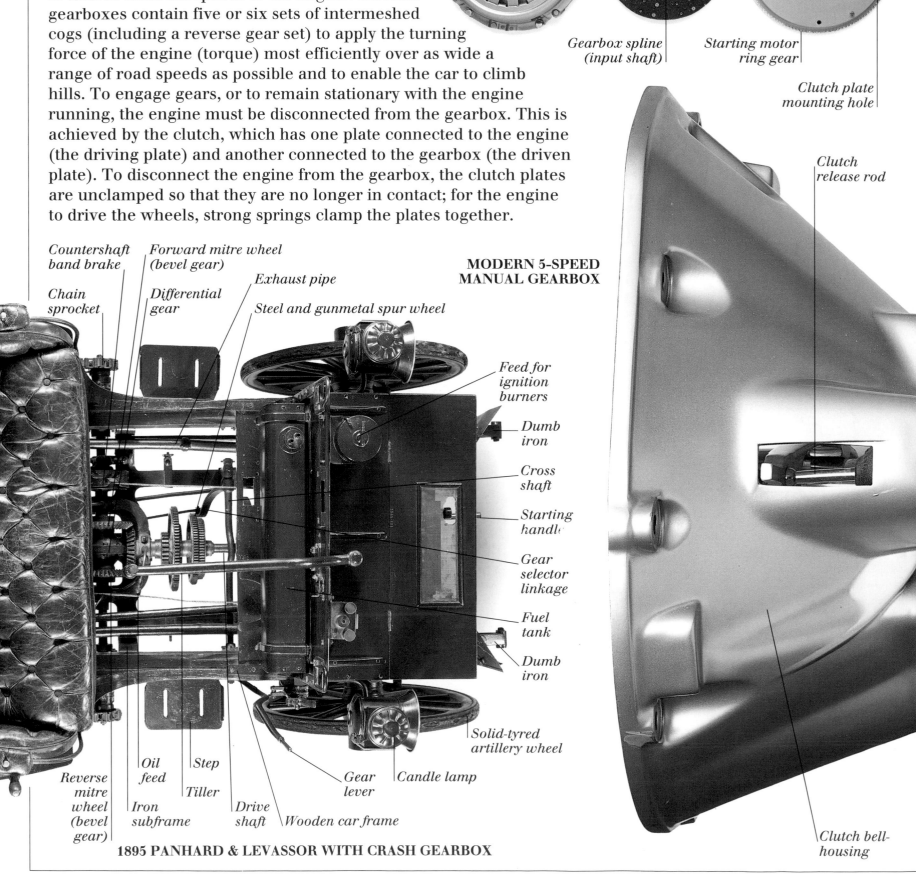

MODERN FRICTION CLUTCH ASSEMBLY

DRIVING PLATE (PRESSURE PLATE)

Leaf spring

DRIVEN PLATE

Rivet

Heat-resistant lining

FLYWHEEL

Crankshaft bolt hole

Gearbox spline (input shaft)

Starting motor ring gear

Clutch plate mounting hole

Clutch release rod

MODERN 5-SPEED MANUAL GEARBOX

Feed for ignition burners

Dumb iron

Cross shaft

Starting handle

Gear selector linkage

Fuel tank

Dumb iron

Clutch bellhousing

Countershaft band brake

Forward mitre wheel (bevel gear)

Exhaust pipe

Differential gear

Steel and gunmetal spur wheel

Chain sprocket

Reverse mitre wheel (bevel gear)

Oil feed

Step

Tiller

Iron subframe

Drive shaft

Wooden car frame

Gear lever

Candle lamp

Solid-tyred artillery wheel

1895 PANHARD & LEVASSOR WITH CRASH GEARBOX

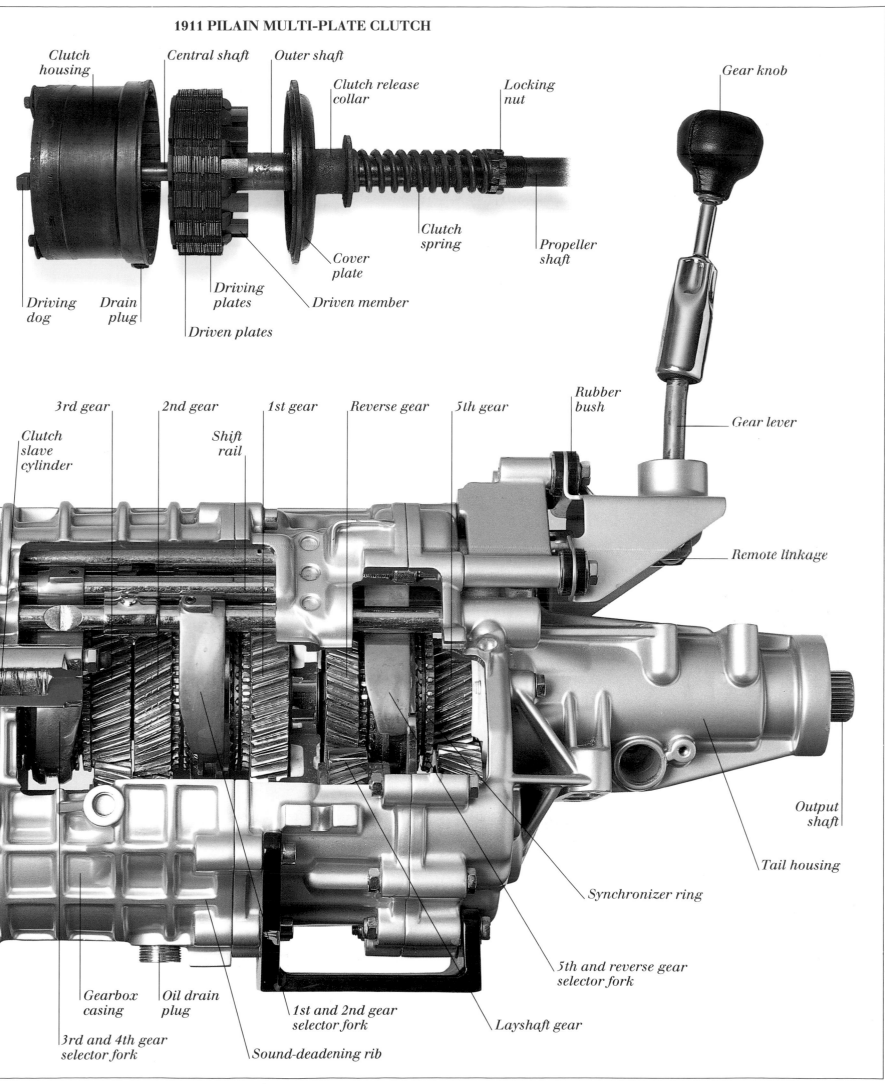

1911 PILAIN MULTI-PLATE CLUTCH

Clutch housing

Central shaft

Outer shaft

Clutch release collar

Locking nut

Gear knob

Clutch spring

Propeller shaft

Cover plate

Driven member

Driving plates

Driven plates

Driving dog

Drain plug

Gear lever

Rubber bush

3rd gear

2nd gear

1st gear

Reverse gear

5th gear

Clutch slave cylinder

Shift rail

Remote linkage

Output shaft

Tail housing

Synchronizer ring

5th and reverse gear selector fork

1st and 2nd gear selector fork

Layshaft gear

Gearbox casing

Oil drain plug

3rd and 4th gear selector fork

Sound-deadening rib

29

Alternative transmissions

THE TRANSMISSION SYSTEM transmits the engine's power to the wheels. Early cars used chains or belts to achieve this, whereas modern cars use a clutch, gearbox, and drive shafts. Some modern cars have a continuously variable transmission, in which a belt runs between pulleys that expand and contract automatically to provide the right gearing ratio. The most common type of automatic gearbox contains planetary gear sets that are selected according to engine speed and throttle opening. Perhaps the most unusual form of transmission was that of the French Leyat, which had no clutch, gearbox, or final drive but was powered by a variable-speed propeller.

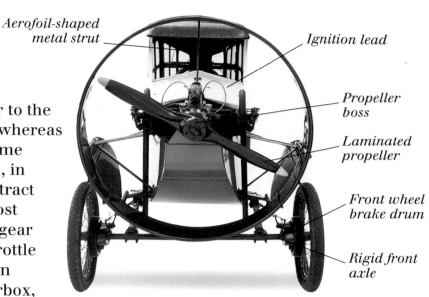

FRONT VIEW OF LEYAT, c.1924

Aerofoil-shaped metal strut

Ignition lead

Propeller boss

Laminated propeller

Front wheel brake drum

Rigid front axle

SIDE VIEW OF LEYAT

Fuselage

Rear mudguard

Steering cabane

Beaded edge tyre

Airscrew shield (propeller shield)

Flat twin engine

Wire wheel

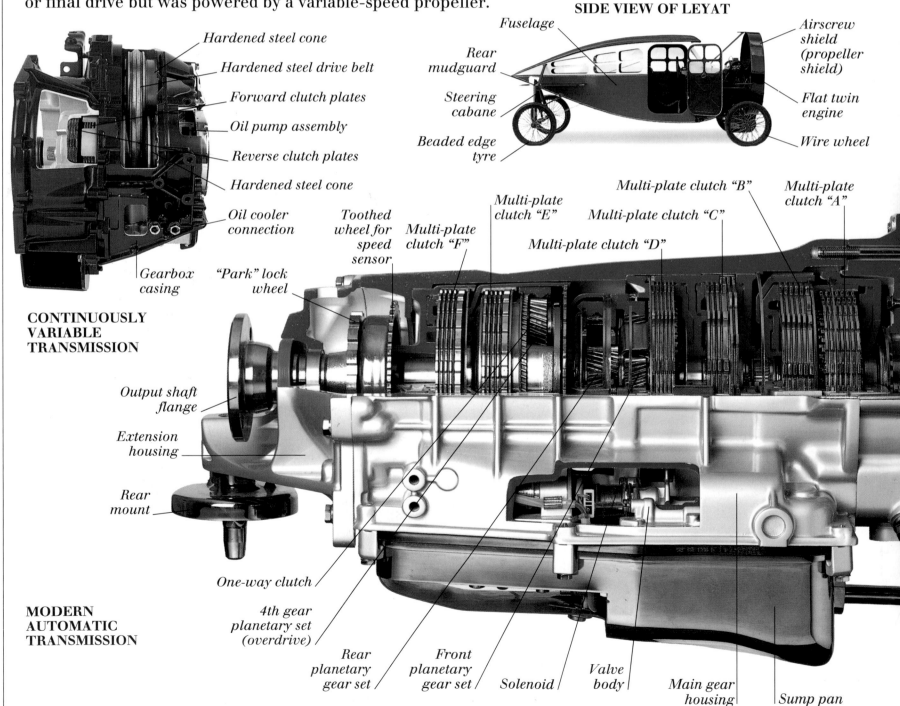

Hardened steel cone

Hardened steel drive belt

Forward clutch plates

Oil pump assembly

Reverse clutch plates

Hardened steel cone

Oil cooler connection

Gearbox casing

CONTINUOUSLY VARIABLE TRANSMISSION

Toothed wheel for speed sensor

"Park" lock wheel

Multi-plate clutch "F"

Multi-plate clutch "E"

Multi-plate clutch "D"

Multi-plate clutch "C"

Multi-plate clutch "B"

Multi-plate clutch "A"

Output shaft flange

Extension housing

Rear mount

One-way clutch

MODERN AUTOMATIC TRANSMISSION

4th gear planetary set (overdrive)

Rear planetary gear set

Front planetary gear set

Solenoid

Valve body

Main gear housing

Sump pan

CHAIN-DRIVEN 70-HP MERCEDES, 1904

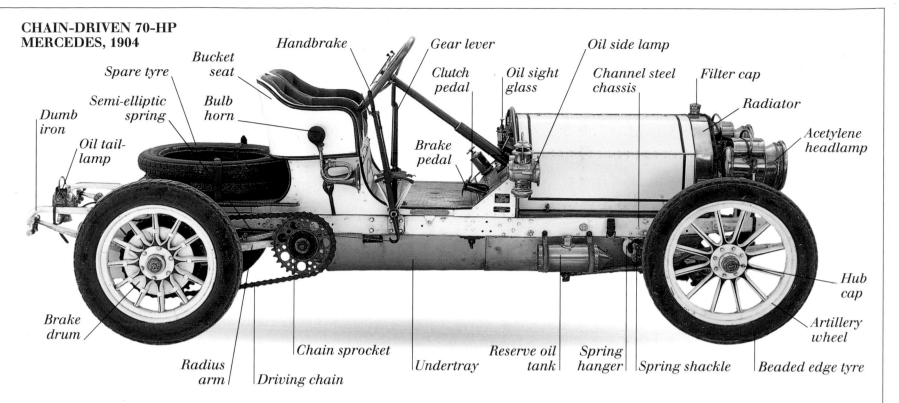

Dumb iron
Oil tail-lamp
Spare tyre
Semi-elliptic spring
Bucket seat
Bulb horn
Handbrake
Gear lever
Clutch pedal
Oil sight glass
Oil side lamp
Channel steel chassis
Filter cap
Radiator
Acetylene headlamp
Brake pedal
Brake drum
Radius arm
Driving chain
Chain sprocket
Undertray
Reserve oil tank
Spring hanger
Spring shackle
Hub cap
Artillery wheel
Beaded edge tyre

BELT-DRIVEN DAIMLER MAYBACH, 1895

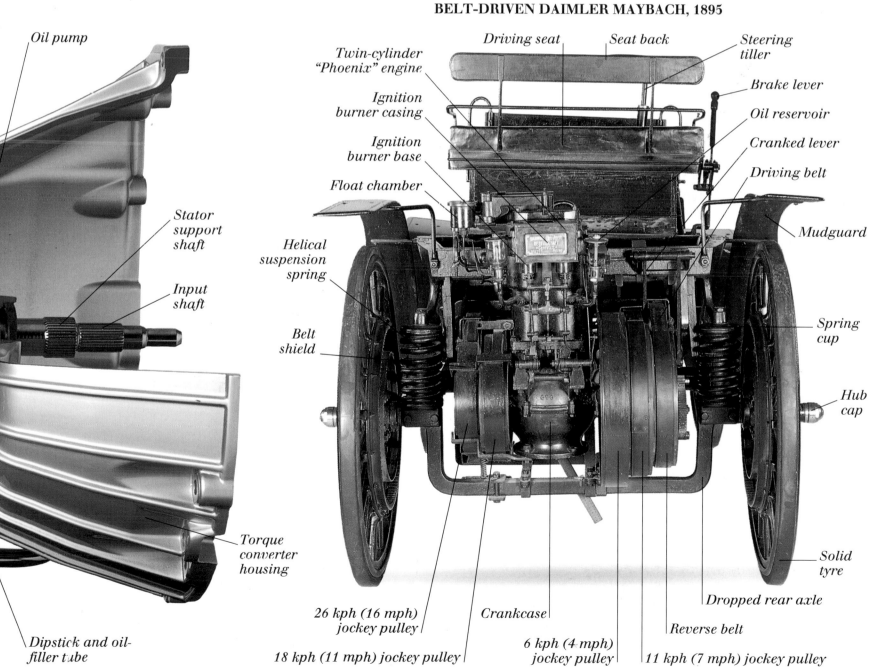

Oil pump
Stator support shaft
Input shaft
Torque converter housing
Dipstick and oil-filler tube

Twin-cylinder "Phoenix" engine
Ignition burner casing
Ignition burner base
Float chamber
Helical suspension spring
Belt shield
Driving seat
Seat back
Steering tiller
Brake lever
Oil reservoir
Cranked lever
Driving belt
Mudguard
Spring cup
Hub cap
Solid tyre
26 kph (16 mph) jockey pulley
18 kph (11 mph) jockey pulley
Crankcase
6 kph (4 mph) jockey pulley
Reverse belt
11 kph (7 mph) jockey pulley
Dropped rear axle

31

Final drive and steering

Drive shaft

Gearbox

MOST EARLY CARS USED THE PANHARD transmission system, named after the manufacturer René Panhard, in which a front-mounted engine drove the rear wheels through a multiple-ratio gearbox. Since the 1960s, most cars have used front-wheel drive, although now powerful cars increasingly use four-wheel drive for its better road-holding. Whatever the drive system used, a driven axle is turned by a final-drive gear, usually located in the gearbox in front-wheel-drive cars. The final-drive gear incorporates a differential gear that allows the outer wheel to turn faster than the inner when driving around corners. In most cars, only the front wheels are steered. The steering column is joined by a pinion to a rack. When the steering wheel is turned, the pinion rolls the rack either right or left, so turning the wheels. Some cars have power-assisted steering, in which hydraulic power makes it easier for the driver to turn the steering wheel. A few cars have steering on all four wheels. The four-wheel-steering rack shown here has an electronic control unit that controls the direction of the rear wheels, while the front wheels are steered conventionally.

**FRONT VIEW OF A
FOUR-WHEEL-DRIVE
RENAULT ESPACE**

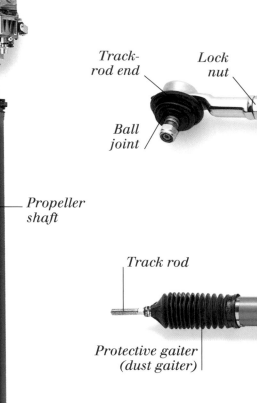

Track-rod end

Lock nut

Ball joint

Propeller shaft

Track rod

Protective gaiter (dust gaiter)

**FOUR-WHEEL-DRIVE
RUNNING GEAR**

Aerodynamic windscreen

"Monobox" body

Rear axle

Differential gear unit

Drive shaft

Brake assembly

**SIDE VIEW OF A FOUR-WHEEL-
DRIVE RENAULT ESPACE**

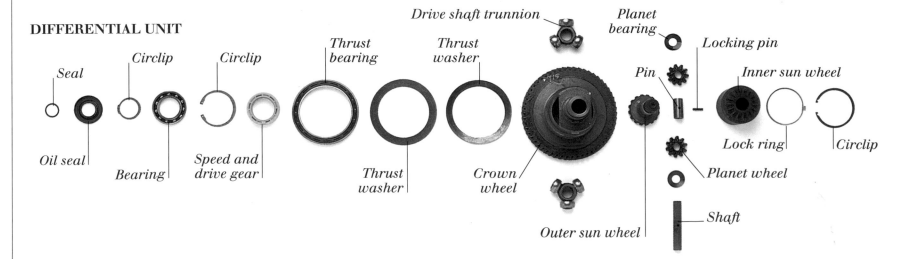

DIFFERENTIAL UNIT

Drive shaft trunnion

Planet bearing

Locking pin

Seal

Circlip

Circlip

Thrust bearing

Thrust washer

Pin

Inner sun wheel

Oil seal

Bearing

Speed and drive gear

Thrust washer

Crown wheel

Lock ring

Circlip

Planet wheel

Shaft

Outer sun wheel

32

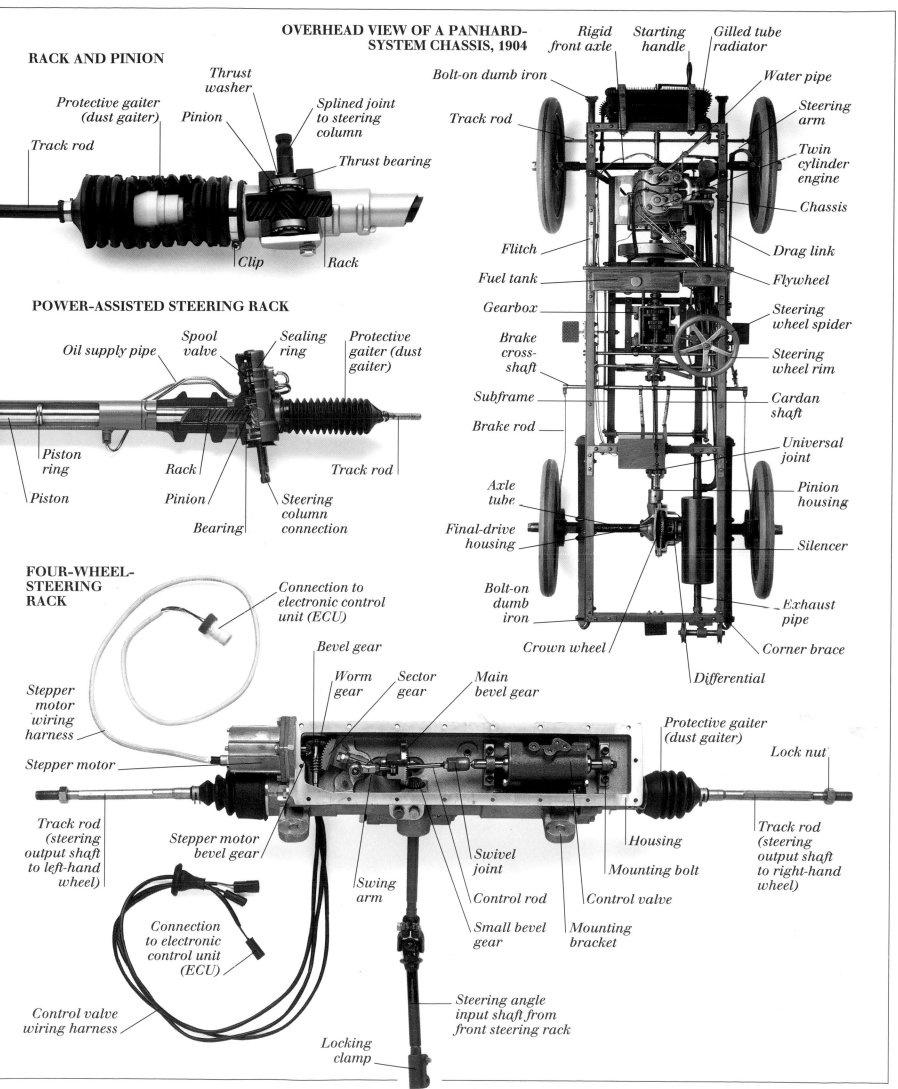

RACK AND PINION

Protective gaiter (dust gaiter)

Track rod

Pinion

Thrust washer

Splined joint to steering column

Thrust bearing

Clip

Rack

OVERHEAD VIEW OF A PANHARD-SYSTEM CHASSIS, 1904

Rigid front axle

Starting handle

Gilled tube radiator

Bolt-on dumb iron

Water pipe

Track rod

Steering arm

Twin cylinder engine

Chassis

Flitch

Drag link

Fuel tank

Flywheel

Gearbox

Steering wheel spider

Brake cross-shaft

Steering wheel rim

Subframe

Cardan shaft

Brake rod

Universal joint

Axle tube

Pinion housing

Final-drive housing

Silencer

Bolt-on dumb iron

Exhaust pipe

Crown wheel

Corner brace

Differential

POWER-ASSISTED STEERING RACK

Oil supply pipe

Spool valve

Sealing ring

Protective gaiter (dust gaiter)

Piston ring

Rack

Track rod

Piston

Pinion

Steering column connection

Bearing

FOUR-WHEEL-STEERING RACK

Connection to electronic control unit (ECU)

Bevel gear

Worm gear

Sector gear

Main bevel gear

Protective gaiter (dust gaiter)

Stepper motor wiring harness

Lock nut

Stepper motor

Track rod (steering output shaft to left-hand wheel)

Stepper motor bevel gear

Swing arm

Swivel joint

Small bevel gear

Control rod

Mounting bracket

Control valve

Housing

Mounting bolt

Track rod (steering output shaft to right-hand wheel)

Connection to electronic control unit (ECU)

Control valve wiring harness

Steering angle input shaft from front steering rack

Locking clamp

Suspension

TWIN TRAILING ARM INDEPENDENT FRONT SUSPENSION

SUSPENSION CUSHIONS THE CAR from the effects of irregular road surfaces. It also helps to maintain maximum contact between the tyres and the road, and so is necessary for effective steering, braking, and acceleration. The earliest suspension systems – leaf springs made of layers of steel leaves – are still used in some cars. However, most modern cars use coil springs, which, unlike leaf springs, have no built-in damping to eliminate unwanted bouncing over rough surfaces; coil springs therefore require separate hydraulic or gas-filled dampers (shock absorbers) to counteract this bouncing. The MacPherson strut is an independent system that combines shock absorbers and a king pin (which acts as a bearing for the steering movement) in one unit. The de Dion system was invented a century ago, but is still used in some modern sports cars because it reduces wheel spin and gives better road-holding.

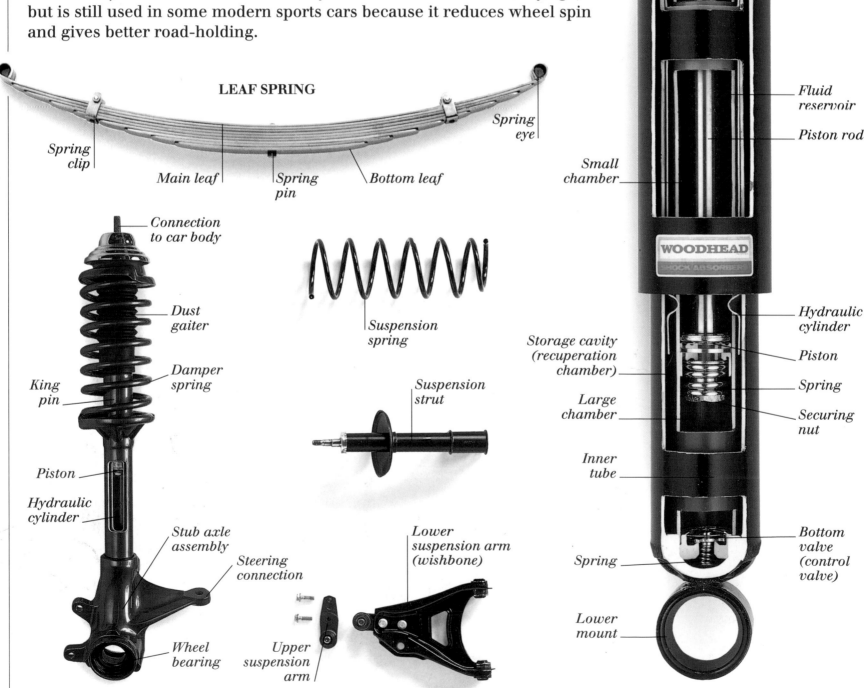

TELESCOPIC HYDRAULIC SHOCK ABSORBER, 1967

Chassis attachment eye (upper mount)

Outer tube

Fluid reservoir

Piston rod

Small chamber

Storage cavity (recuperation chamber)

Large chamber

Inner tube

Spring

Hydraulic cylinder

Piston

Spring

Securing nut

Bottom valve (control valve)

Lower mount

LEAF SPRING

Spring eye

Spring clip

Main leaf

Spring pin

Bottom leaf

Connection to car body

Dust gaiter

Damper spring

King pin

Piston

Hydraulic cylinder

Stub axle assembly

Steering connection

Wheel bearing

Suspension spring

Suspension strut

Lower suspension arm (wishbone)

Upper suspension arm

MACPHERSON STRUT

COIL AND WISHBONE SUSPENSION

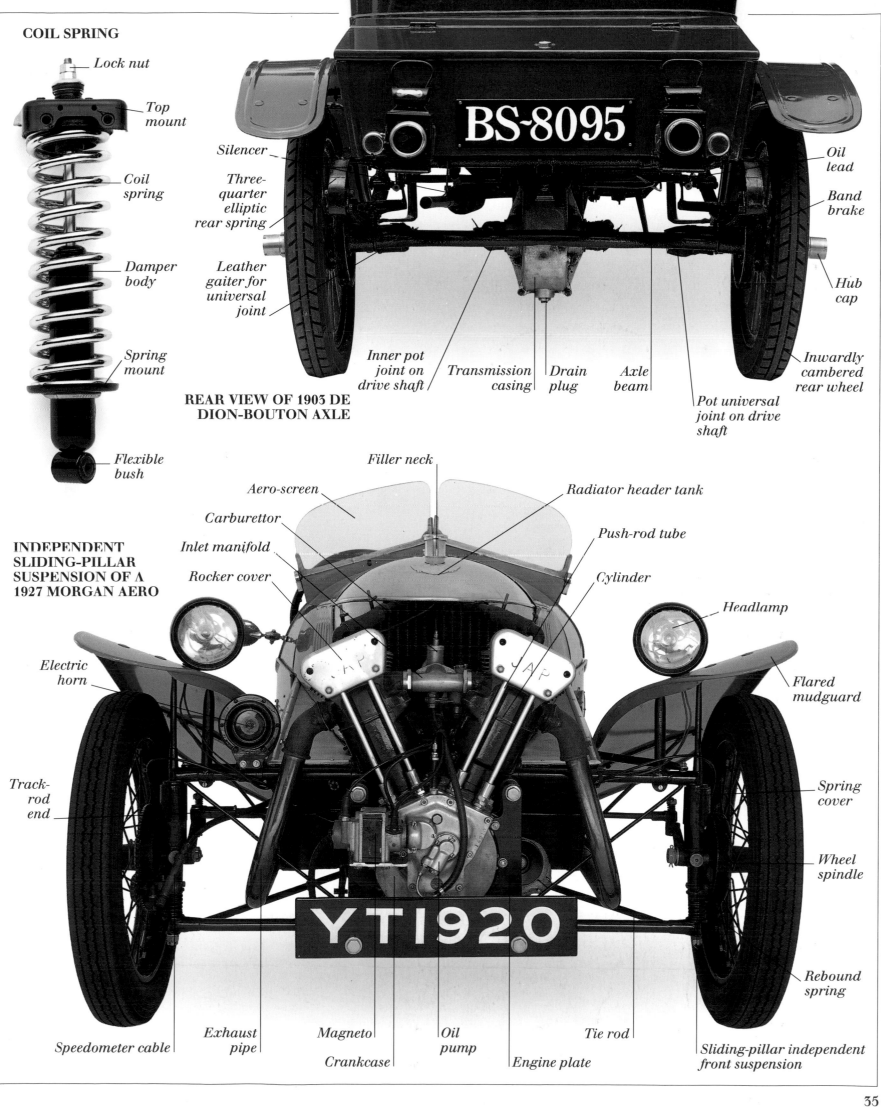

COIL SPRING

Lock nut

Top mount

Coil spring

Damper body

Spring mount

Flexible bush

Silencer

Three-quarter elliptic rear spring

Leather gaiter for universal joint

Inner pot joint on drive shaft

Transmission casing

Drain plug

Axle beam

Pot universal joint on drive shaft

Oil lead

Band brake

Hub cap

Inwardly cambered rear wheel

REAR VIEW OF 1903 DE DION-BOUTON AXLE

INDEPENDENT SLIDING-PILLAR SUSPENSION OF A 1927 MORGAN AERO

Filler neck

Aero-screen

Carburettor

Inlet manifold

Rocker cover

Radiator header tank

Push-rod tube

Cylinder

Headlamp

Electric horn

Flared mudguard

Track-rod end

Spring cover

Wheel spindle

Rebound spring

Speedometer cable

Exhaust pipe

Magneto

Crankcase

Oil pump

Engine plate

Tie rod

Sliding-pillar independent front suspension

BS·8095

Y T I 9 2 0

Wheels and tyres

IT IS NOT ENOUGH FOR A CAR WHEEL SIMPLY TO BE ROUND; it must also be strong enough to withstand violent stresses, and carefully balanced so that it rotates evenly. It must be light yet stiff so that it does not affect the steering and suspension, and must allow air to flow over and cool the brakes. Early cars had wooden-spoked wheels, as did horse-drawn carriages, but such wheels can be distorted by heavy loads and by shrinkage. Wire wheels, derived from bicycle wheels, effectively hang the car from the wheel rim by precisely-tensioned thin spokes. The simplest form of modern wheel is the pressed steel disc, while cast aluminium wheels permit wider (low-profile) tyres to be fitted for better grip (see pp. 46-47). The first tyres were made from solid rubber but they were superseded by pneumatic (air-filled) tyres, which provided a more comfortable ride. A major advance came with the introduction of radial-ply tyres in the 1950s – their flexible sidewalls give better cornering and longer tread life.

"BIBENDUM", TRADEMARK OF THE MICHELIN TYRE COMPANY

HUB

Bolt-on plate

Spoke hole

Splines / Thread

"Knock-off" nut

Dowel

Rounded tongue to enter felloe

Belly

ARTILLERY WHEEL (WOODEN-SPOKED WHEEL)

Face of spoke

Knock

Spoke

Felloe

Bolt hole for hub

Ring of felloes

Hole for spoke

TYPES OF TYRE

METAL-STUDDED NON-SKID, ITALY, 1914

RUBBER-STUDDED, FRANCE, 1926

EXTRA-FORT, ITALY, 1911

CONFORT BIBENDUM, FRANCE, 1928

CABLE, ITALY, 1919

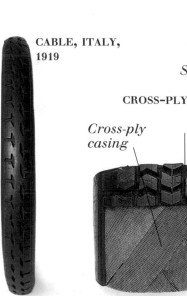

CROSS-PLY

Cross-ply casing

Tread groove

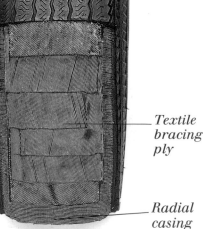

TEXTILE-BRACED RADIAL

Shoulder

Sidewall

Sipes

Textile bracing ply

Radial casing

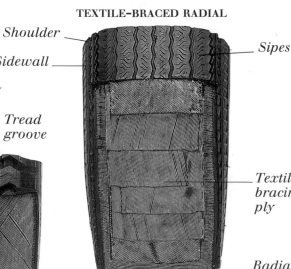

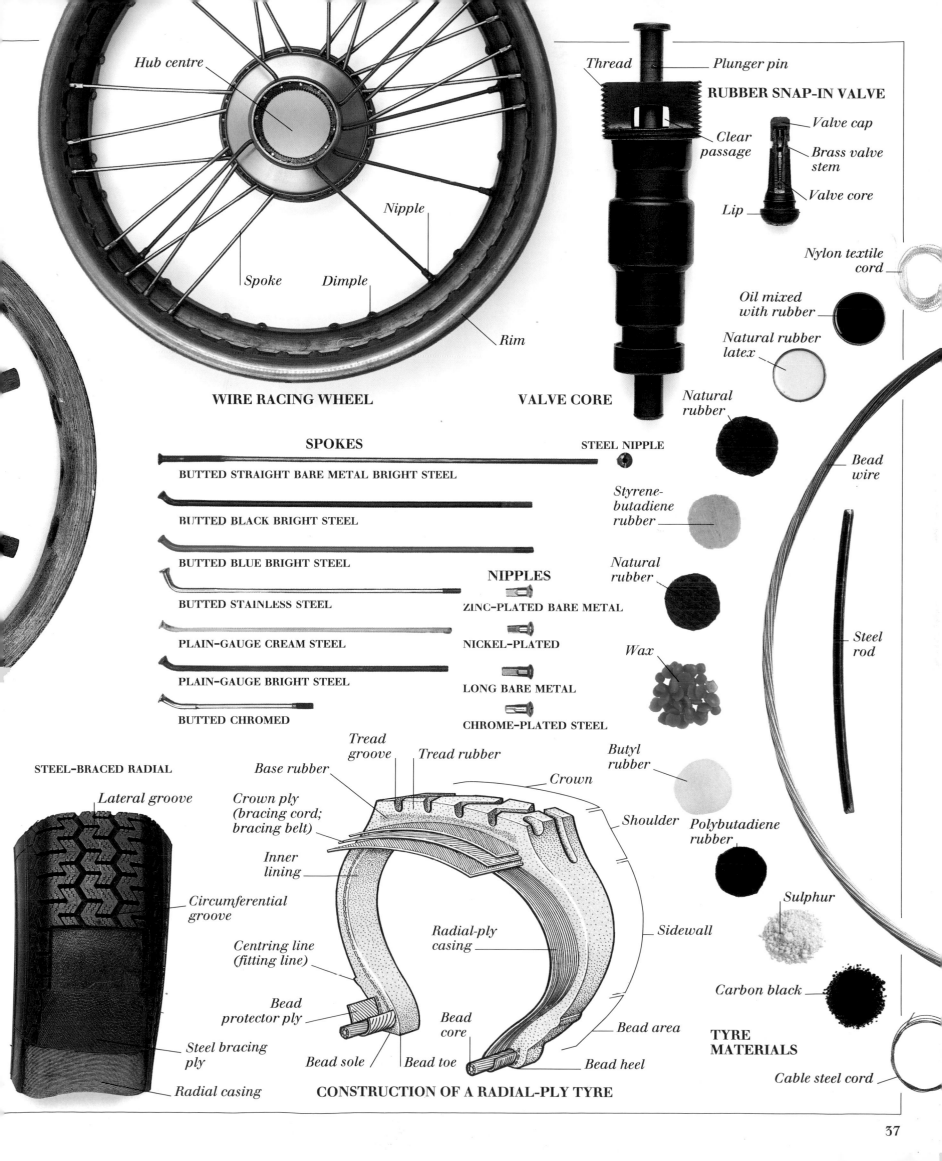

Hub centre

Nipple

Spoke   Dimple

Rim

WIRE RACING WHEEL

Thread   Plunger pin

RUBBER SNAP-IN VALVE

Clear
passage

Valve cap

Brass valve
stem

Valve core

Lip

VALVE CORE

Nylon textile
cord

Oil mixed
with rubber

Natural rubber
latex

Natural
rubber

Bead
wire

SPOKES

STEEL NIPPLE

BUTTED STRAIGHT BARE METAL BRIGHT STEEL

BUTTED BLACK BRIGHT STEEL

Styrene-
butadiene
rubber

BUTTED BLUE BRIGHT STEEL

Natural
rubber

Steel
rod

BUTTED STAINLESS STEEL

NIPPLES

ZINC-PLATED BARE METAL

PLAIN-GAUGE CREAM STEEL

NICKEL-PLATED

Wax

PLAIN-GAUGE BRIGHT STEEL

LONG BARE METAL

BUTTED CHROMED

CHROME-PLATED STEEL

Butyl
rubber

STEEL-BRACED RADIAL

Tread
groove

Tread rubber

Lateral groove

Base rubber

Crown

Crown ply
(bracing cord;
bracing belt)

Shoulder

Polybutadiene
rubber

Inner
lining

Circumferential
groove

Radial-ply
casing

Centring line
(fitting line)

Sidewall

Sulphur

Bead
protector ply

Bead
core

Carbon black

**TYRE
MATERIALS**

Bead area

Steel bracing
ply

Bead sole   Bead toe

Bead heel

Radial casing

CONSTRUCTION OF A RADIAL-PLY TYRE

Cable steel cord

Brakes

BRAKES WERE A WEAK POINT of early cars, because they often exerted uneven pressure on the wheels, causing the vehicle to pull to one side. Many early cars had wrap-around band brakes, but they performed poorly in the wet. Drum brakes (brake shoes that expand internally in a drum) on all four wheels became standard in the 1920s, but when used repeatedly, such brakes "fade" (when heat distorts the drums), leading to temporary loss of braking power. The solution – discovered in the 1950s – was to use disc brakes, in which brake pads press against a heat-conducting metal disc. Now, cars use drum brakes only on the rear wheels, and disc brakes on the front or on all four wheels.

MODERN DRUM BRAKE

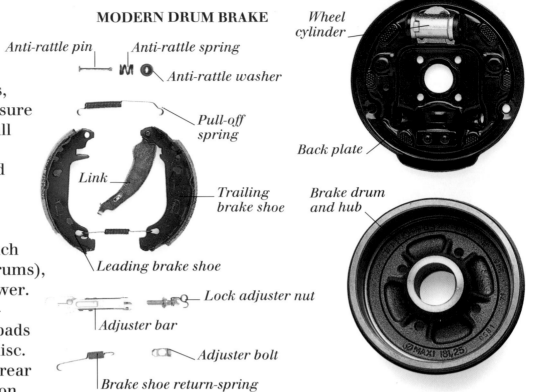

Anti-rattle pin
Anti-rattle spring
Anti-rattle washer
Pull-off spring
Link
Trailing brake shoe
Leading brake shoe
Lock adjuster nut
Adjuster bar
Adjuster bolt
Brake shoe return-spring
Wheel cylinder
Back plate
Brake drum and hub

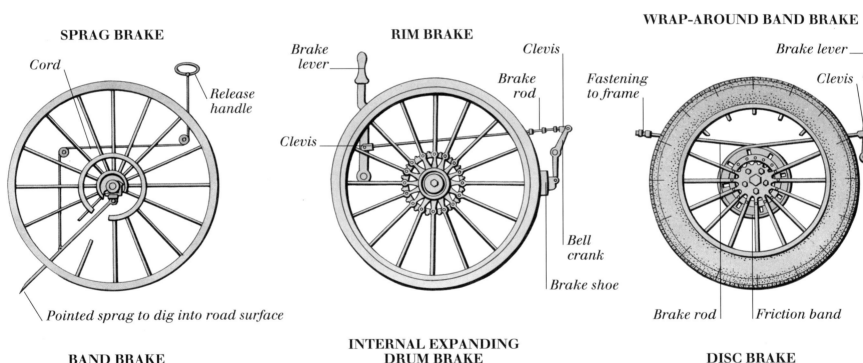

SPRAG BRAKE

Cord
Release handle
Pointed sprag to dig into road surface

RIM BRAKE

Brake lever
Clevis
Brake rod
Clevis
Bell crank
Brake shoe

WRAP-AROUND BAND BRAKE

Brake lever
Clevis
Fastening to frame
Brake rod
Friction band

BAND BRAKE

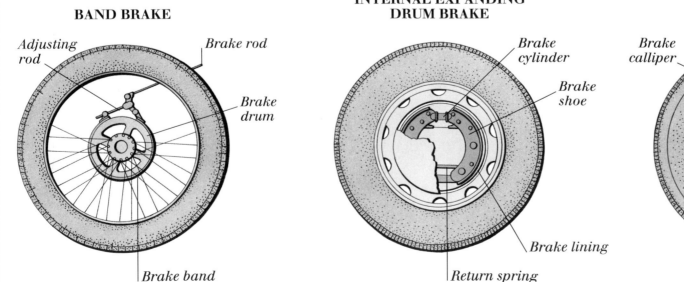

Adjusting rod
Brake rod
Brake drum
Brake band

INTERNAL EXPANDING DRUM BRAKE

Brake cylinder
Brake shoe
Brake lining
Return spring

DISC BRAKE

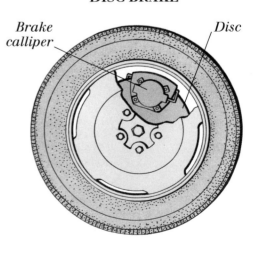

Brake calliper
Disc

MODERN FRONT WHEEL DISC BRAKE

FRONT AND REAR VIEWS OF ANTI-LOCK BRAKING SYSTEM

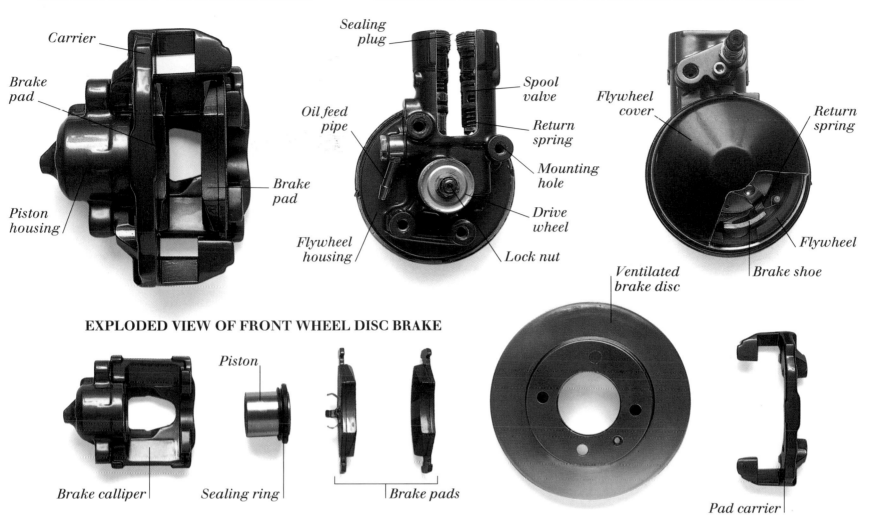

Carrier

Brake pad

Piston housing

Brake pad

Sealing plug

Oil feed pipe

Spool valve

Return spring

Mounting hole

Flywheel housing

Drive wheel

Lock nut

Flywheel cover

Return spring

Flywheel

Brake shoe

EXPLODED VIEW OF FRONT WHEEL DISC BRAKE

Piston

Brake calliper

Sealing ring

Brake pads

Ventilated brake disc

Pad carrier

MARKUS MOTOR CARRIAGE WITH WOODEN BLOCK BRAKES, 1887

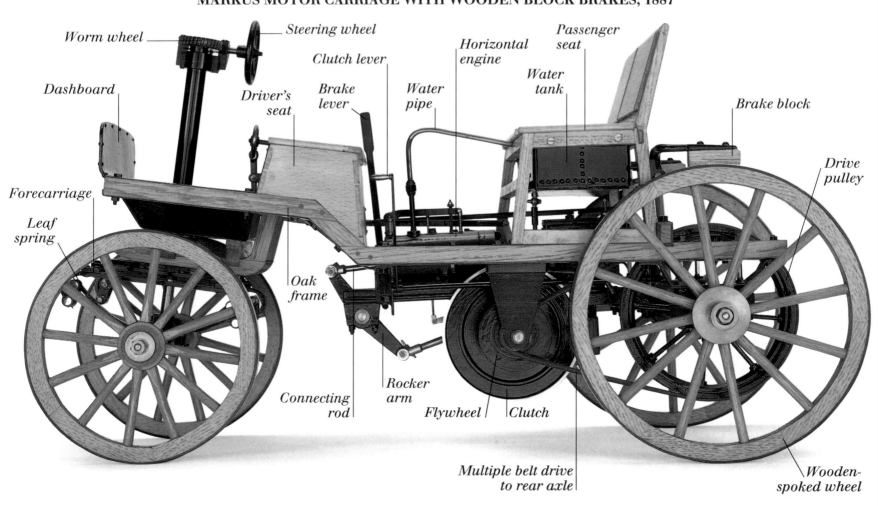

Worm wheel

Steering wheel

Clutch lever

Horizontal engine

Passenger seat

Dashboard

Brake lever

Water pipe

Water tank

Driver's seat

Brake block

Forecarriage

Drive pulley

Leaf spring

Oak frame

Connecting rod

Rocker arm

Flywheel

Clutch

Multiple belt drive to rear axle

Wooden-spoked wheel

Instruments

THE FIRST CARS REQUIRED such frequent attention to fuel, water, and lubricants that no instruments were necessary. The 1904 Mercedes (below) has a "brake-and-gradient meter" for indicating the efficiency of the car, but no speedometer. As the performance of cars improved, speed indicators, like the Cowey and Bowden meters shown here, appeared. The Cowey could also record the speed travelled at points 50 yards apart over the previous 750 yards. Soon, simple fuel and water gauges were added. Modern instrument panels monitor performance using electronic, rather than mechanical means. Their read-outs are often digital, as shown right.

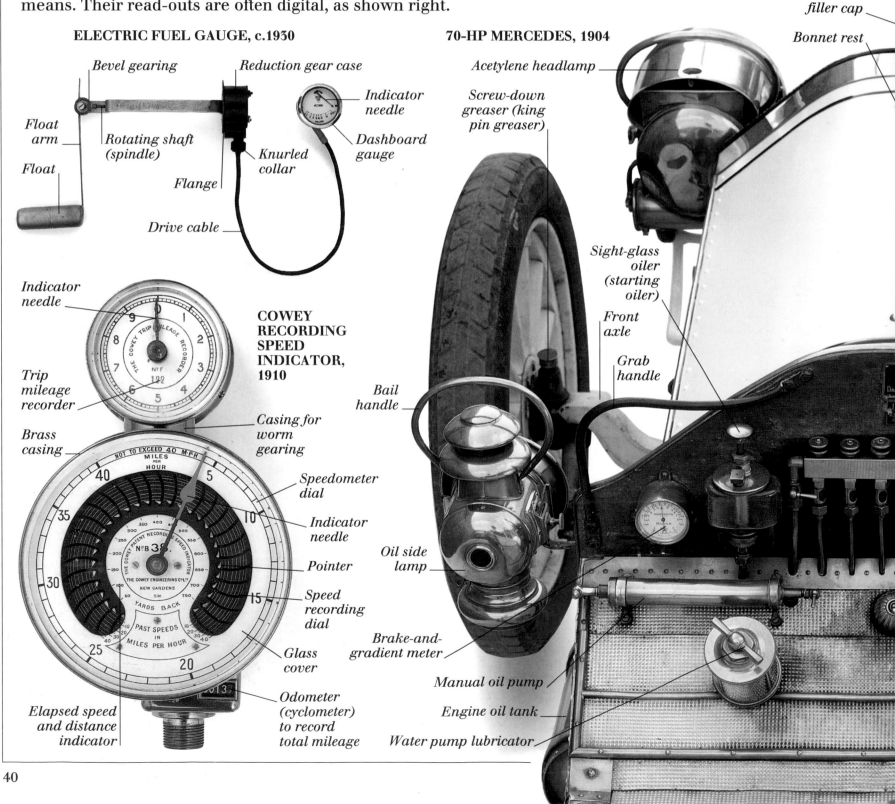

Fascia air vent · Clock · Battery-charge gauge · Oil-level gauge · Tachometer (revolution counter)

Stereo control panel · Fan control dial · Heater control · Ventilation control · Fuel-level gauge · Water-temperature gauge · Speedometer

ELECTRIC FUEL GAUGE, c.1930

Bevel gearing · Reduction gear case · Indicator needle · Dashboard gauge · Float arm · Rotating shaft (spindle) · Knurled collar · Flange · Float · Drive cable

COWEY RECORDING SPEED INDICATOR, 1910

Indicator needle · Trip mileage recorder · Brass casing · Casing for worm gearing · Speedometer dial · Indicator needle · Pointer · Speed recording dial · Glass cover · Odometer (cyclometer) to record total mileage · Elapsed speed and distance indicator

THE COWEY TRIP MILEAGE RECORDER

NOT TO EXCEED 40 M.P.H · MILES PER HOUR · THE COWEY PATENT RECORDING SPEED INDICATOR · THE COWEY ENGINEERING CO.LTD · KEW GARDENS · S.W. · YARDS BACK · PAST SPEEDS IN MILES PER HOUR

70-HP MERCEDES, 1904

Radiator filler cap · Bonnet rest · Acetylene headlamp · Screw-down greaser (king pin greaser) · Sight-glass oiler (starting oiler) · Front axle · Grab handle · Bail handle · Oil side lamp · Brake-and-gradient meter · Manual oil pump · Engine oil tank · Water pump lubricator

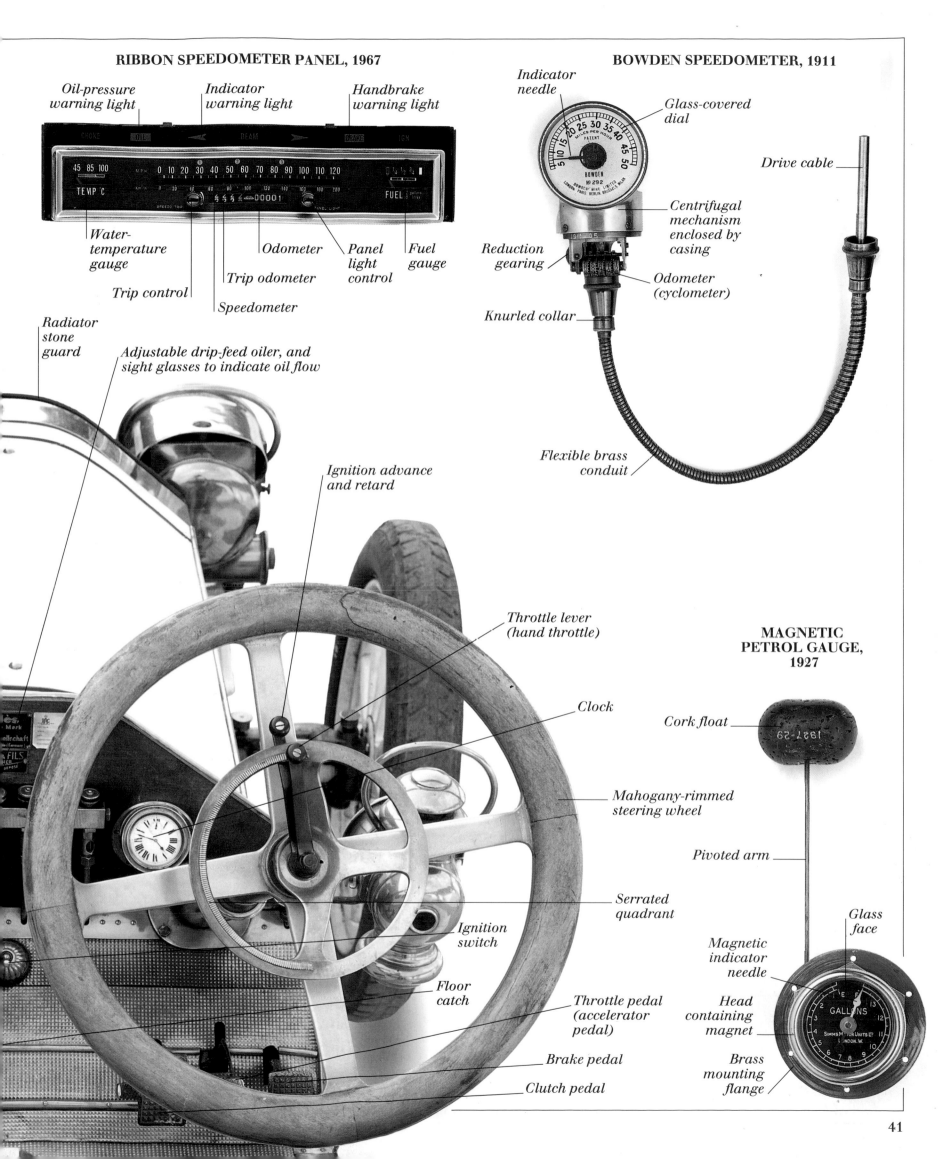

RIBBON SPEEDOMETER PANEL, 1967

Oil-pressure warning light

Indicator warning light

Handbrake warning light

Water-temperature gauge

Trip control

Trip odometer

Speedometer

Odometer

Panel light control

Fuel gauge

BOWDEN SPEEDOMETER, 1911

Indicator needle

Glass-covered dial

Drive cable

Centrifugal mechanism enclosed by casing

Reduction gearing

Odometer (cyclometer)

Knurled collar

Flexible brass conduit

Radiator stone guard

Adjustable drip-feed oiler, and sight glasses to indicate oil flow

Ignition advance and retard

Throttle lever (hand throttle)

MAGNETIC PETROL GAUGE, 1927

Cork float

Clock

Mahogany-rimmed steering wheel

Pivoted arm

Serrated quadrant

Ignition switch

Floor catch

Throttle pedal (accelerator pedal)

Brake pedal

Clutch pedal

Glass face

Magnetic indicator needle

Head containing magnet

Brass mounting flange

Electrical systems

THE FIRST USE OF ELECTRICITY in cars was small batteries used to power the ignition system. The first electric headlamps appeared in 1905 and gradually superseded those using acetylene gas. Electricity is used extensively in modern cars; lighting, ignition, locking, windows, stereo systems, instruments, and alarms are all controlled electrically, and are linked to the power source by a complex wiring loom. Today, electrical systems often incorporate computers, which may control various functions, even including adjusting the position of the driver's seat to suit the needs of individual drivers.

MERCEDES COMPUTERIZED ELECTRIC SEAT

Drive belt
Back release
Backrest release
Seat belt
Drive cable
Head restraint motor
Back-lock motor
Runner
Gearbox
Gearbox and backrest adjustment motor
Fire extinguisher mounting bracket
Front seat lift
Main control loom

DRIP-FEED ACETYLENE GENERATOR, 1911

Lid for carbide chamber
Retaining nut
Carbide chamber
Water chamber

WIRING LOOM OF A MODERN CAR

Left-hand rear lamp
Rear lamps harness
Number-plate lamp
Right-hand rear lamp
Rear windscreen heater and boot-lamp harness

Rear wiper harness
Left-hand rear shelf speaker
Right-hand rear shelf speaker
Aerial
Wiper switch

Door radio speaker
Fuse board assembly
Fuse box
Lighting switch
Dash harness
Instrument panel assembly
Right-hand side harness

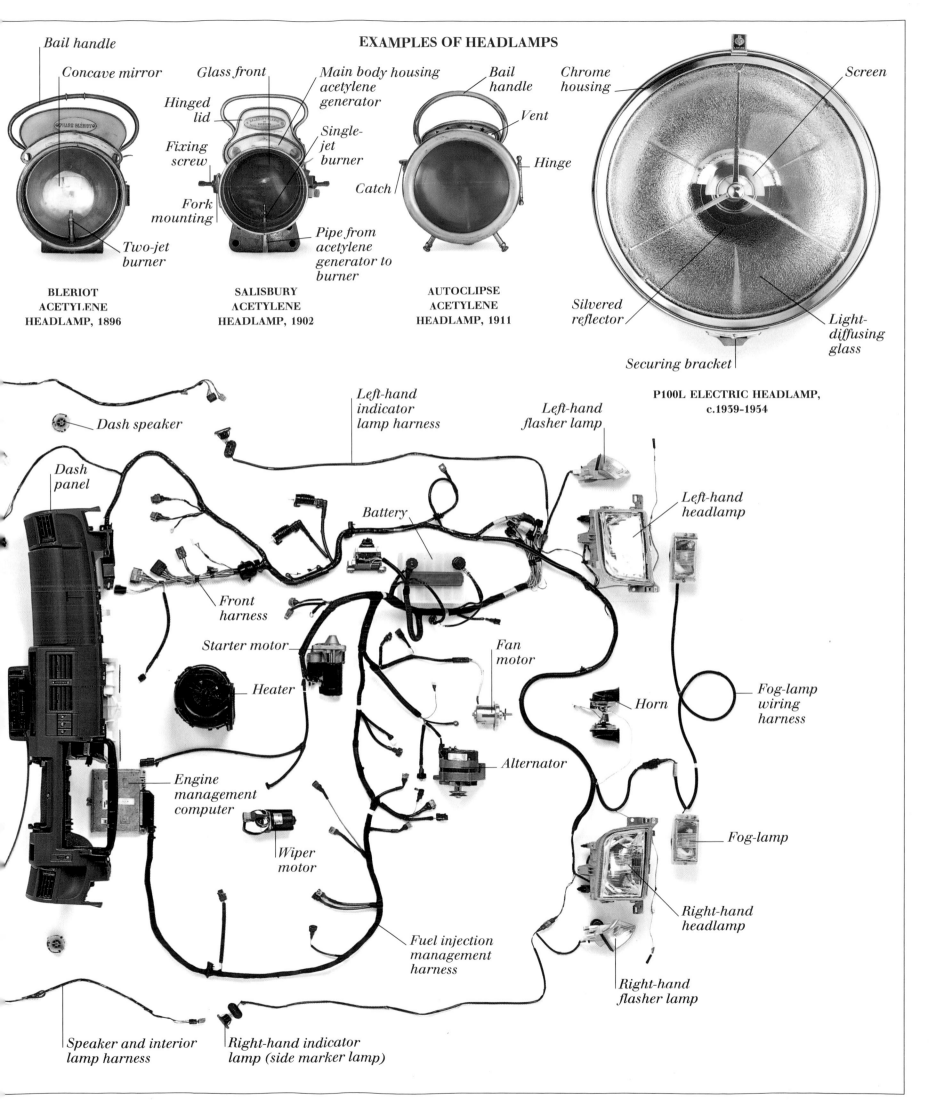

EXAMPLES OF HEADLAMPS

Bail handle

Concave mirror

**BLERIOT
ACETYLENE
HEADLAMP, 1896**

Two-jet burner

Glass front

Hinged lid

Fixing screw

Fork mounting

Main body housing acetylene generator

Single-jet burner

Pipe from acetylene generator to burner

**SALISBURY
ACETYLENE
HEADLAMP, 1902**

Bail handle

Vent

Hinge

Catch

**AUTOCLIPSE
ACETYLENE
HEADLAMP, 1911**

Chrome housing

Screen

Silvered reflector

Light-diffusing glass

Securing bracket

**P100L ELECTRIC HEADLAMP,
c.1939–1954**

Dash speaker

Dash panel

Front harness

Starter motor

Heater

Engine management computer

Wiper motor

Left-hand indicator lamp harness

Battery

Left-hand flasher lamp

Left-hand headlamp

Fan motor

Horn

Fog-lamp wiring harness

Fog-lamp

Alternator

Right-hand headlamp

Fuel injection management harness

Right-hand flasher lamp

Speaker and interior lamp harness

Right-hand indicator lamp (side marker lamp)

Modern bodywork

THE BODY OF A MODERN MASS-PRODUCED CAR is built on the monocoque (single-shell) principle, in which the roof, side panels, and floor are welded into a single integral unit. This bodyshell protects and supports the car's internal parts. Steel and glass are used to construct the bodyshell, creating a unit that is both light and strong. Its lightness helps to conserve energy, while its strength protects the occupants. Modern bodywork is designed with the aid of computers, which are used to predict factors such as aerodynamic efficiency and impact-resistance. High-technology is also employed on the production line, where robots are used to assemble, weld, and paint the body.

RENAULT LOGO

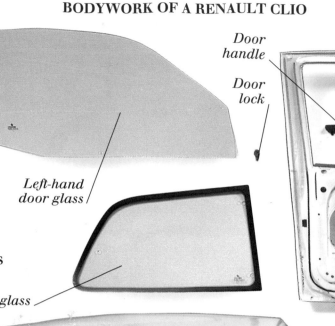

Door handle

Door lock

Left-hand door glass

Left-hand quarter glass

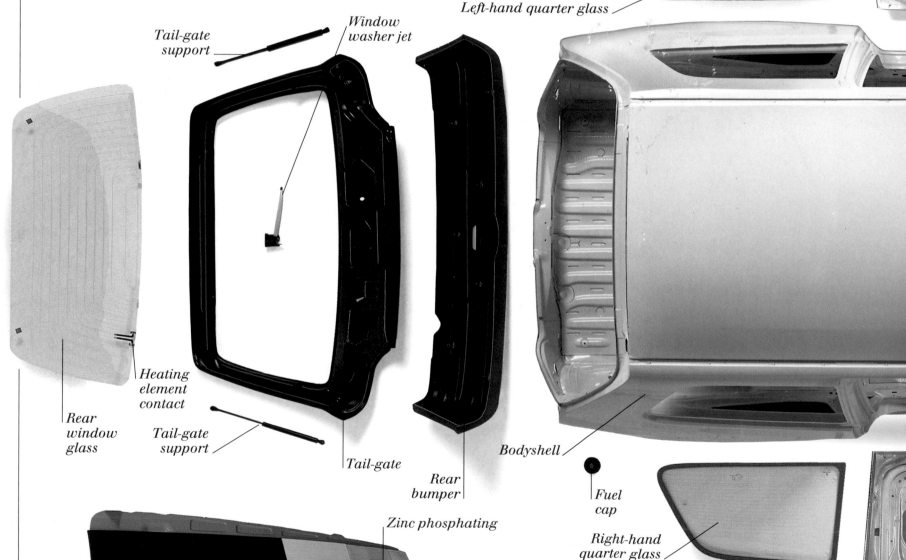

Tail-gate support

Window washer jet

Rear window glass

Heating element contact

Tail-gate support

Tail-gate

Rear bumper

Bodyshell

Fuel cap

Right-hand quarter glass

Right-hand door glass

Door key and lock

Door handle

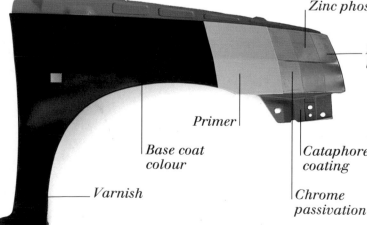

Zinc phosphating

Degreased bare metal

Primer

Base coat colour

Cataphoresic coating

Varnish

Chrome passivation

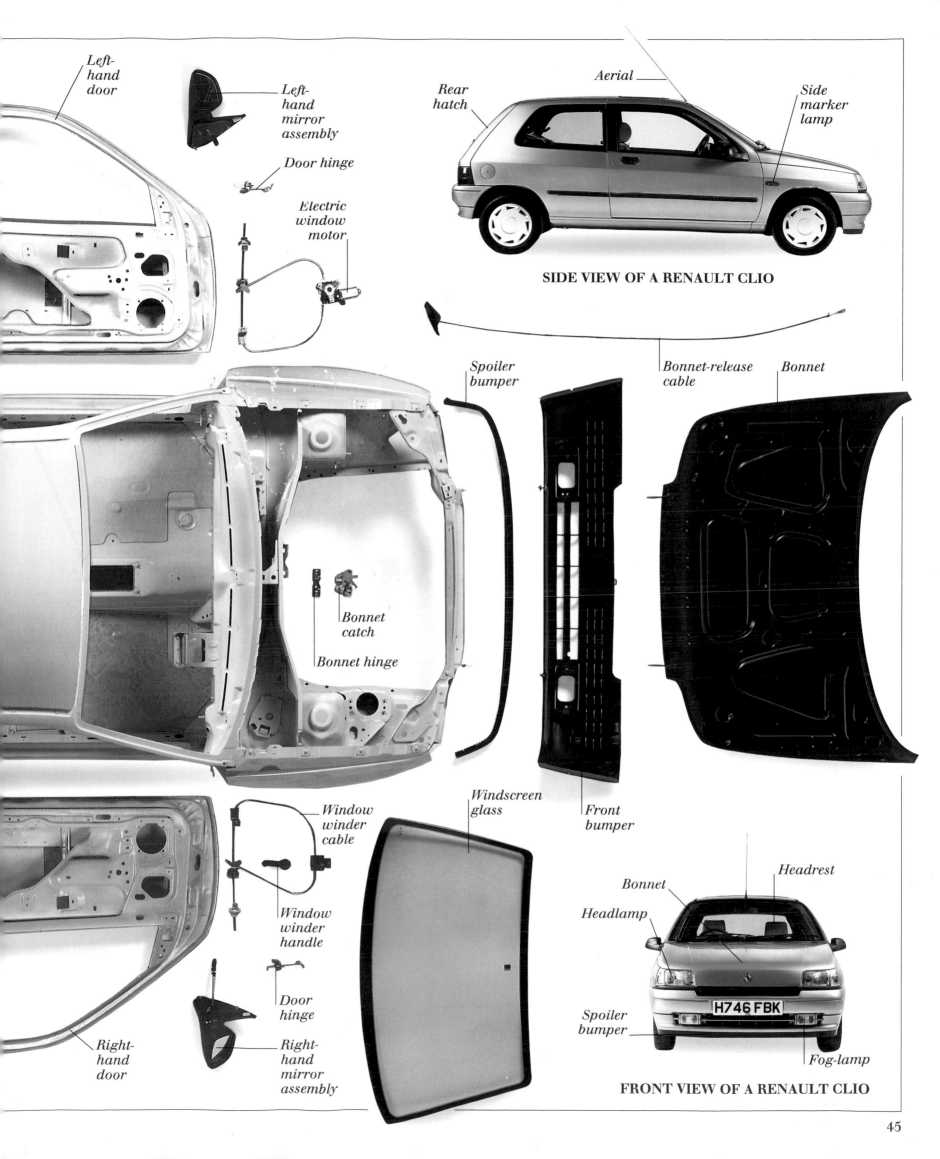

Left-hand door

Left-hand mirror assembly

Door hinge

Electric window motor

Aerial

Rear hatch

Side marker lamp

SIDE VIEW OF A RENAULT CLIO

Bonnet-release cable

Bonnet

Spoiler bumper

Bonnet catch

Bonnet hinge

Windscreen glass

Front bumper

Window winder cable

Window winder handle

Door hinge

Right-hand door

Right-hand mirror assembly

Headrest

Bonnet

Headlamp

Spoiler bumper

Fog-lamp

H746 FBK

FRONT VIEW OF A RENAULT CLIO

45

Modern mechanics

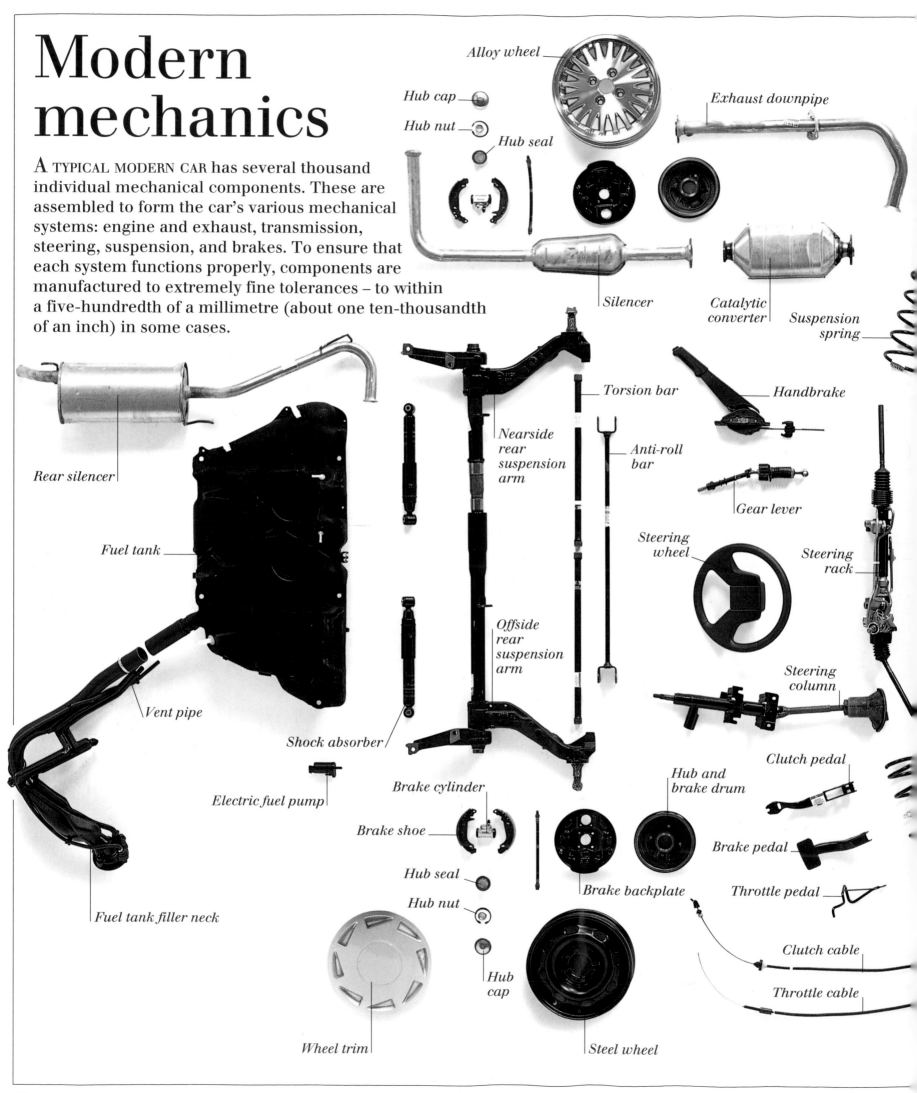

A TYPICAL MODERN CAR has several thousand individual mechanical components. These are assembled to form the car's various mechanical systems: engine and exhaust, transmission, steering, suspension, and brakes. To ensure that each system functions properly, components are manufactured to extremely fine tolerances – to within a five-hundredth of a millimetre (about one ten-thousandth of an inch) in some cases.

Alloy wheel

Hub cap

Hub nut

Hub seal

Exhaust downpipe

Silencer

Catalytic converter

Suspension spring

Rear silencer

Fuel tank

Vent pipe

Shock absorber

Electric fuel pump

Brake cylinder

Brake shoe

Hub seal

Hub nut

Fuel tank filler neck

Torsion bar

Handbrake

Nearside rear suspension arm

Anti-roll bar

Gear lever

Steering wheel

Steering rack

Offside rear suspension arm

Steering column

Clutch pedal

Hub and brake drum

Brake pedal

Throttle pedal

Brake backplate

Clutch cable

Throttle cable

Wheel trim

Hub cap

Steel wheel

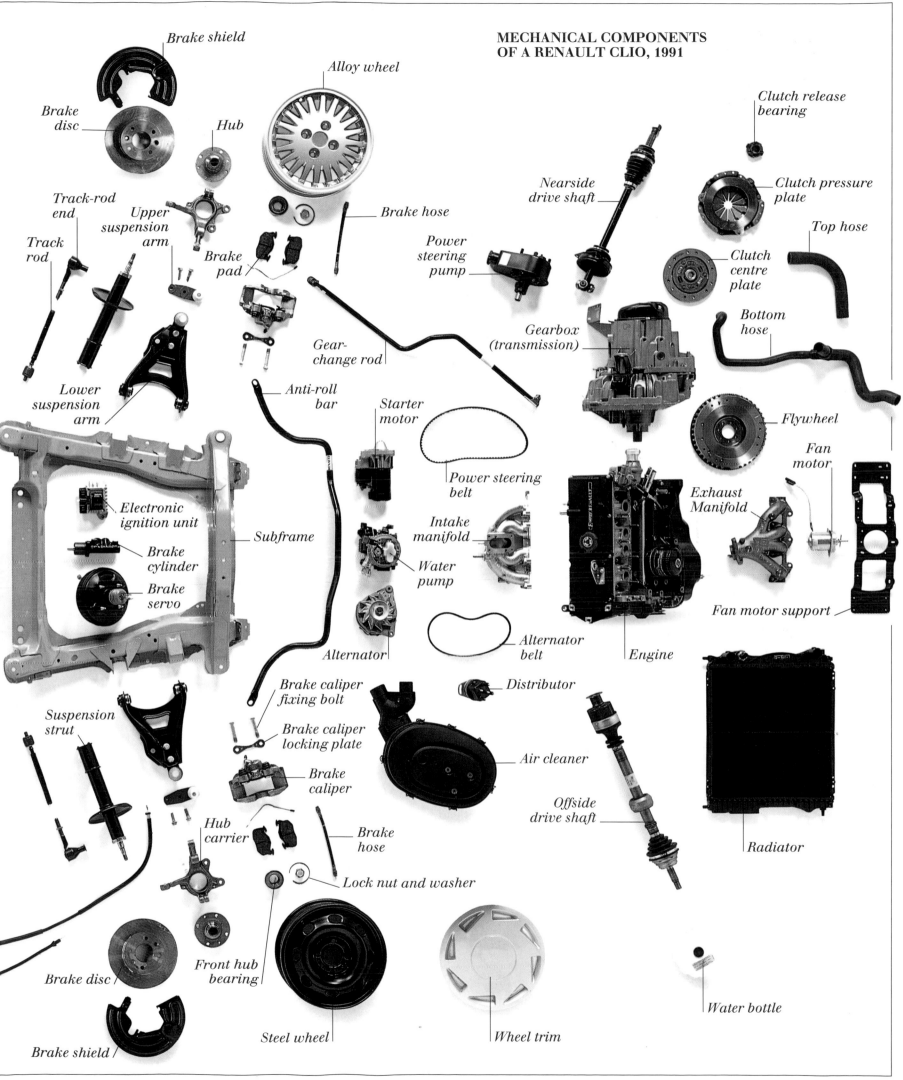

Brake shield

Alloy wheel

Clutch release
bearing

Brake
disc

Hub

Nearside
drive shaft

Clutch pressure
plate

Track-rod
end

Upper
suspension
arm

Brake hose

Power
steering
pump

Top hose

Track
rod

Brake
pad

Clutch
centre
plate

Lower
suspension
arm

Gear-
change rod

Gearbox
(transmission)

Bottom
hose

Anti-roll
bar

Starter
motor

Flywheel

Fan
motor

Electronic
ignition unit

Subframe

Power steering
belt

Exhaust
Manifold

Brake
cylinder

Intake
manifold

Brake
servo

Water
pump

Fan motor support

Alternator
belt

Engine

Suspension
strut

Alternator

Brake caliper
fixing bolt

Distributor

Brake caliper
locking plate

Air cleaner

Brake
caliper

Offside
drive shaft

Hub
carrier

Brake
hose

Radiator

Lock nut and washer

Brake disc

Front hub
bearing

Brake shield

Steel wheel

Wheel trim

Water bottle

Modern trim

A MODERN CAR HAS TWO TYPES OF TRIM, according to the materials used: hard (chrome and plastics) and soft (upholstery materials). Safety and comfort are priorities in the trim's design: seats help the occupants to maintain a comfortable posture, rubber seals keep out dirt and moisture, and headlamps light the way. Older cars had interior or leather panelling cut and fitted by craftsmen; modern cars use precisely moulded plastics and seat fabrics cut by robot-controlled lasers to reduce costs and production time. Doors are now trimmed off the production line so that complex wiring can be built in.

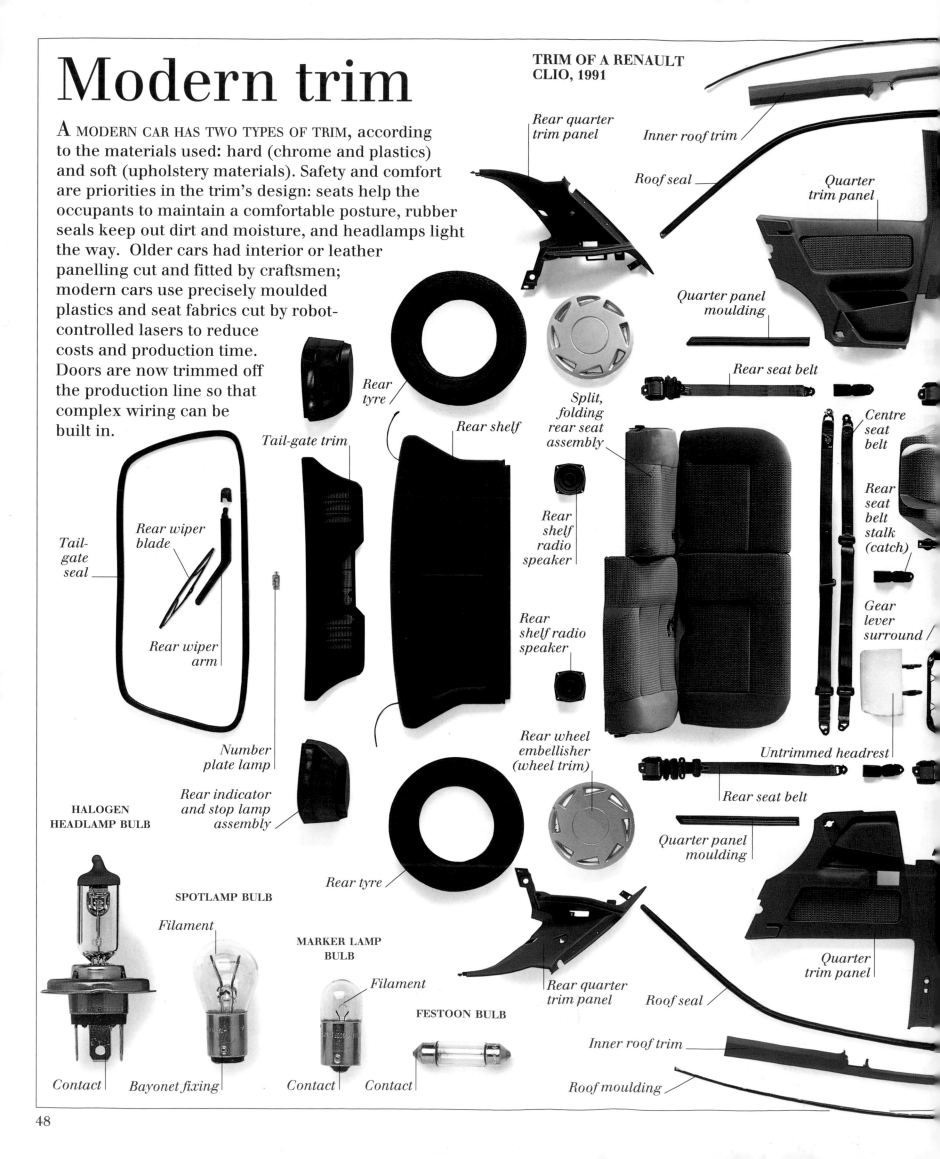

TRIM OF A RENAULT CLIO, 1991

Rear quarter trim panel

Inner roof trim

Roof seal

Quarter trim panel

Quarter panel moulding

Rear tyre

Split, folding rear seat assembly

Rear seat belt

Centre seat belt

Rear seat belt stalk (catch)

Rear shelf

Tail-gate trim

Rear shelf radio speaker

Gear lever surround

Tail-gate seal

Rear wiper blade

Rear wiper arm

Rear shelf radio speaker

Number plate lamp

Rear wheel embellisher (wheel trim)

Untrimmed headrest

Rear indicator and stop lamp assembly

Rear seat belt

HALOGEN HEADLAMP BULB

Rear tyre

Quarter panel moulding

Quarter trim panel

SPOTLAMP BULB

Filament

MARKER LAMP BULB

Rear quarter trim panel

Roof seal

Filament

FESTOON BULB

Inner roof trim

Contact   Bayonet fixing   Contact   Contact

Roof moulding

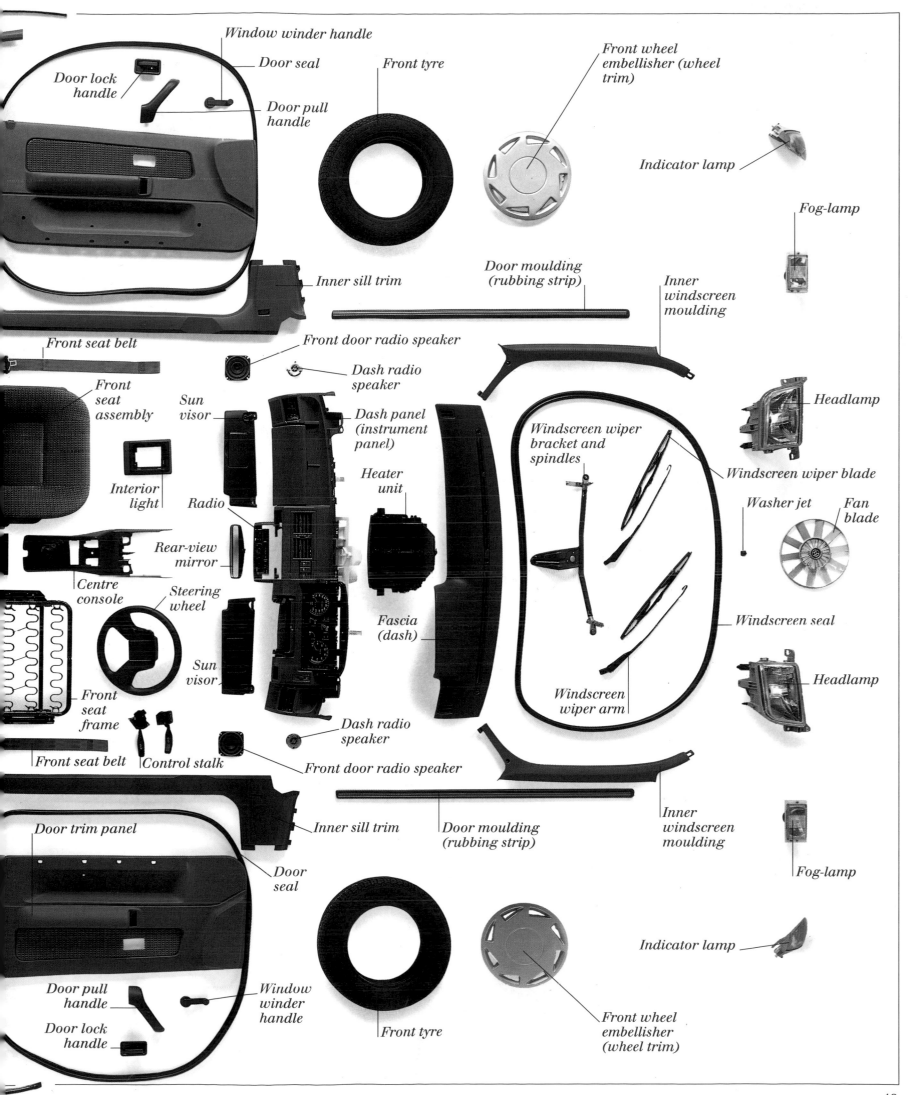

Window winder handle

Door lock handle

Door seal

Door pull handle

Front tyre

Front wheel embellisher (wheel trim)

Indicator lamp

Fog-lamp

Inner sill trim

Door moulding (rubbing strip)

Inner windscreen moulding

Front seat belt

Front door radio speaker

Dash radio speaker

Headlamp

Front seat assembly

Sun visor

Dash panel (instrument panel)

Windscreen wiper bracket and spindles

Windscreen wiper blade

Heater unit

Washer jet

Fan blade

Interior light

Radio

Rear-view mirror

Centre console

Steering wheel

Windscreen seal

Sun visor

Fascia (dash)

Front seat frame

Headlamp

Door trim panel

Dash radio speaker

Windscreen wiper arm

Front seat belt

Control stalk

Front door radio speaker

Inner sill trim

Door moulding (rubbing strip)

Inner windscreen moulding

Fog-lamp

Door seal

Door pull handle

Window winder handle

Door lock handle

Front tyre

Front wheel embellisher (wheel trim)

Indicator lamp

49

Coachbuilt cars

IN THE EARLY DAYS OF MOTORING, the purchasers of high-quality cars bought a chassis and then had a body built to their individual requirements by a craftsman coachbuilder – two examples are the Rolls-Royces on these pages. Early car bodies were built along principles similar to those used in horse-carriage construction, although allowance had to be made for the extra stresses that made one year's use of a motor car equivalent to several of a horse-drawn carriage. For this reason, the wings, running boards, and wooden framework (which was covered by hand-formed wooden or metal panelling) were strengthened by iron stays made by blacksmiths. The bodywork was then finished with many coats of hand-applied paint and varnish.

ASH FRAMES

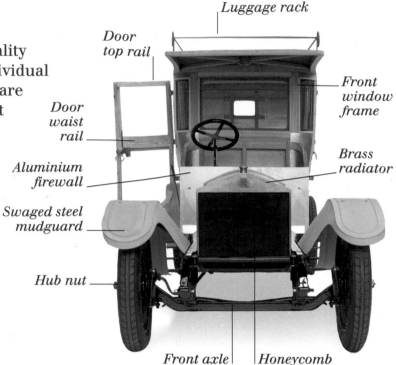

FRONT VIEW OF "D" FRONT LIMOUSINE

Luggage rack

Door top rail

Front window frame

Door waist rail

Brass radiator

Aluminium firewall

Swaged steel mudguard

Hub nut

Front axle

Honeycomb radiator core

1911 ROLLS-ROYCE SILVER GHOST "D" FRONT LIMOUSINE

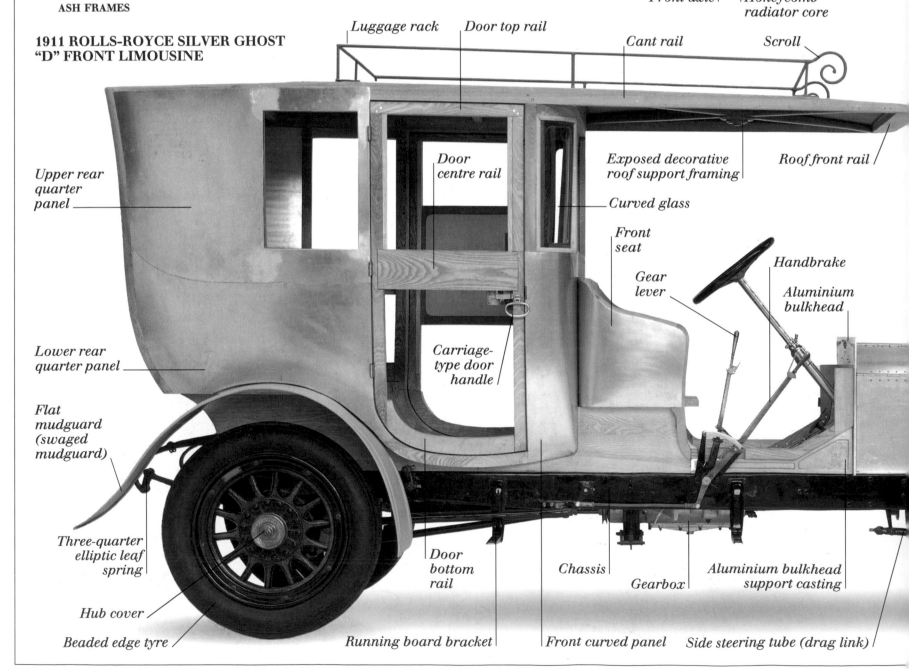

Luggage rack

Door top rail

Cant rail

Scroll

Upper rear quarter panel

Door centre rail

Exposed decorative roof support framing

Roof front rail

Curved glass

Front seat

Handbrake

Gear lever

Aluminium bulkhead

Lower rear quarter panel

Carriage-type door handle

Flat mudguard (swaged mudguard)

Three-quarter elliptic leaf spring

Door bottom rail

Chassis

Aluminium bulkhead support casting

Hub cover

Gearbox

Beaded edge tyre

Running board bracket

Front curved panel

Side steering tube (drag link)

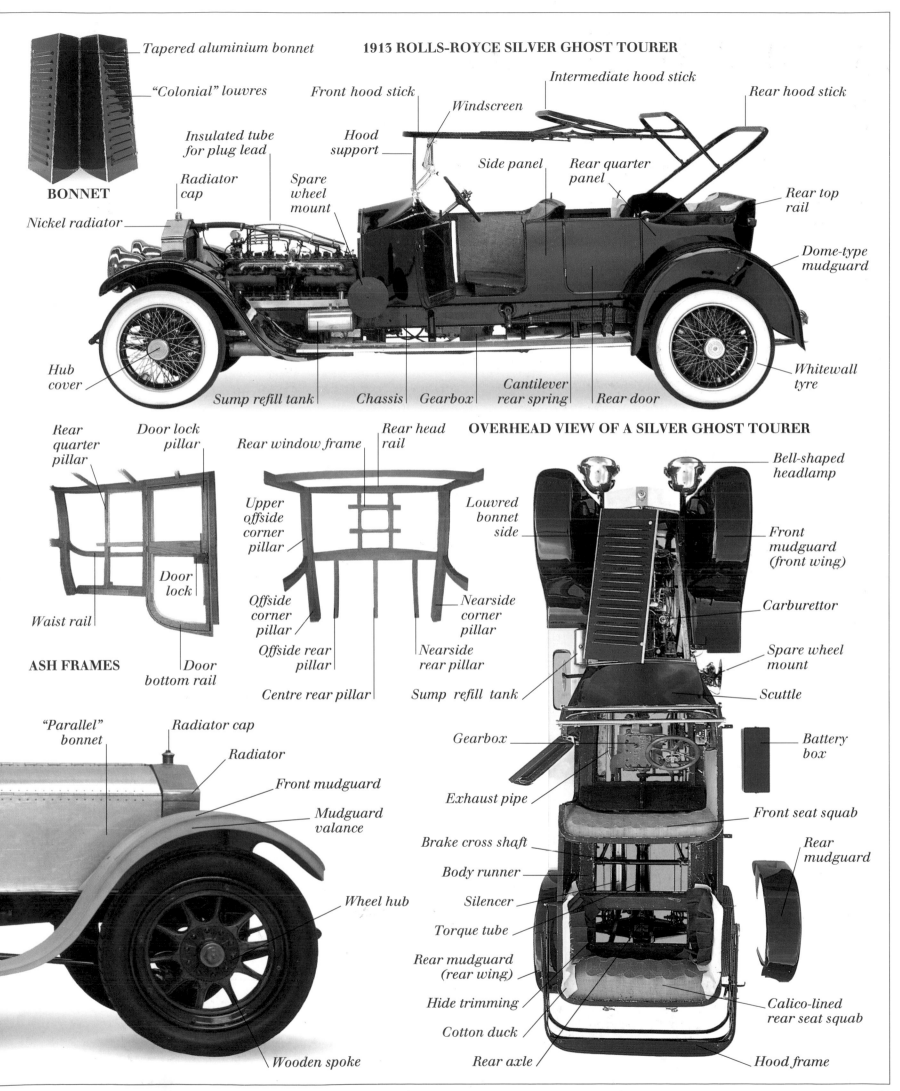

1913 ROLLS-ROYCE SILVER GHOST TOURER

Tapered aluminium bonnet

"Colonial" louvres

BONNET

Insulated tube for plug lead

Radiator cap

Nickel radiator

Front hood stick

Hood support

Windscreen

Intermediate hood stick

Rear hood stick

Spare wheel mount

Side panel

Rear quarter panel

Rear top rail

Dome-type mudguard

Hub cover

Sump refill tank

Chassis

Gearbox

Cantilever rear spring

Rear door

Whitewall tyre

ASH FRAMES

Rear quarter pillar

Door lock pillar

Waist rail

Door lock

Door bottom rail

Rear window frame

Rear head rail

Upper offside corner pillar

Offside corner pillar

Offside rear pillar

Centre rear pillar

Nearside corner pillar

Nearside rear pillar

OVERHEAD VIEW OF A SILVER GHOST TOURER

Louvred bonnet side

Sump refill tank

Bell-shaped headlamp

Front mudguard (front wing)

Carburettor

Spare wheel mount

Scuttle

Gearbox

Exhaust pipe

Battery box

Front seat squab

Brake cross shaft

Body runner

Silencer

Torque tube

Rear mudguard (rear wing)

Hide trimming

Cotton duck

Rear axle

Rear mudguard

Calico-lined rear seat squab

Hood frame

"Parallel" bonnet

Radiator cap

Radiator

Front mudguard

Mudguard valance

Wheel hub

Wooden spoke

Cars assembled by hand

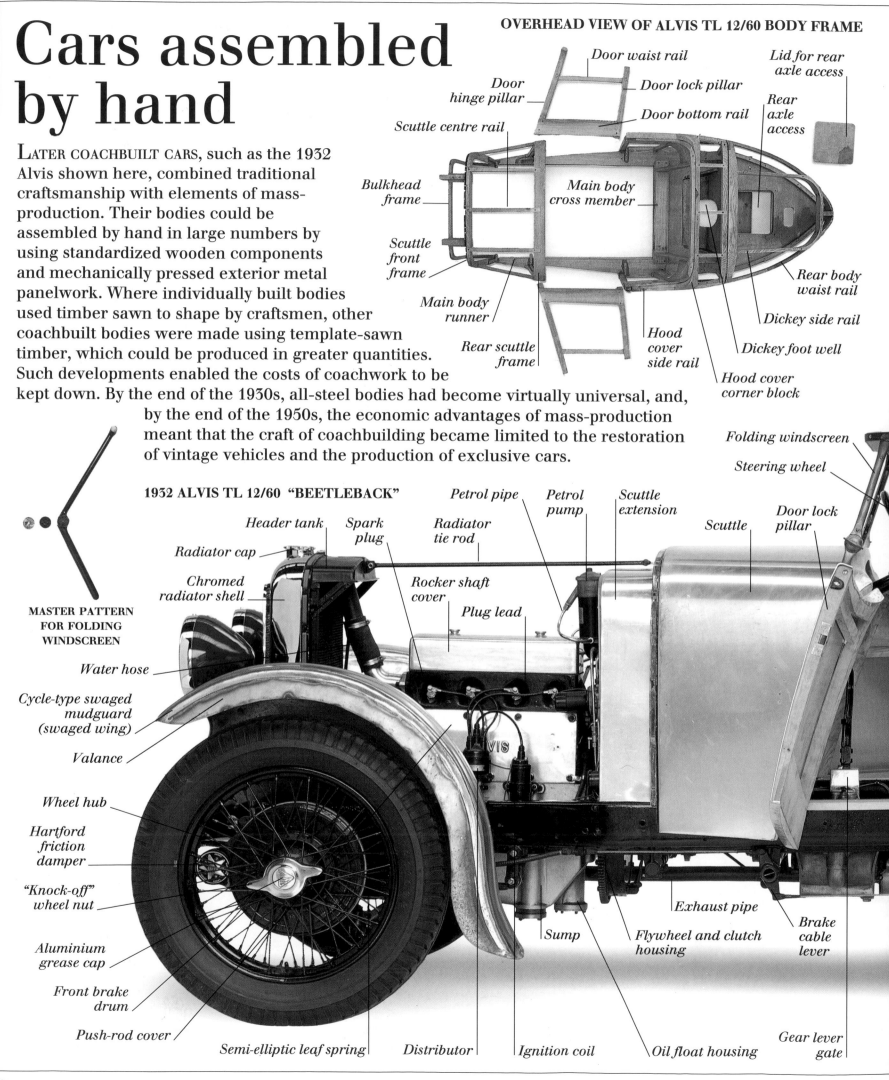

LATER COACHBUILT CARS, such as the 1932 Alvis shown here, combined traditional craftsmanship with elements of mass-production. Their bodies could be assembled by hand in large numbers by using standardized wooden components and mechanically pressed exterior metal panelwork. Where individually built bodies used timber sawn to shape by craftsmen, other coachbuilt bodies were made using template-sawn timber, which could be produced in greater quantities. Such developments enabled the costs of coachwork to be kept down. By the end of the 1930s, all-steel bodies had become virtually universal, and, by the end of the 1950s, the economic advantages of mass-production meant that the craft of coachbuilding became limited to the restoration of vintage vehicles and the production of exclusive cars.

OVERHEAD VIEW OF ALVIS TL 12/60 BODY FRAME

Door waist rail
Door hinge pillar
Door lock pillar
Lid for rear axle access
Scuttle centre rail
Door bottom rail
Rear axle access
Bulkhead frame
Main body cross member
Scuttle front frame
Main body runner
Rear body waist rail
Rear scuttle frame
Hood cover side rail
Dickey side rail
Dickey foot well
Hood cover corner block

1932 ALVIS TL 12/60 "BEETLEBACK"

Petrol pipe
Petrol pump
Scuttle extension
Folding windscreen
Steering wheel
Header tank
Spark plug
Radiator tie rod
Scuttle
Door lock pillar
Radiator cap
Rocker shaft cover
Chromed radiator shell
Plug lead

MASTER PATTERN FOR FOLDING WINDSCREEN

Water hose
Cycle-type swaged mudguard (swaged wing)
Valance
Wheel hub
Hartford friction damper
"Knock-off" wheel nut
Aluminium grease cap
Front brake drum
Push-rod cover
Semi-elliptic leaf spring
Distributor
Ignition coil
Sump
Flywheel and clutch housing
Exhaust pipe
Oil float housing
Brake cable lever
Gear lever gate

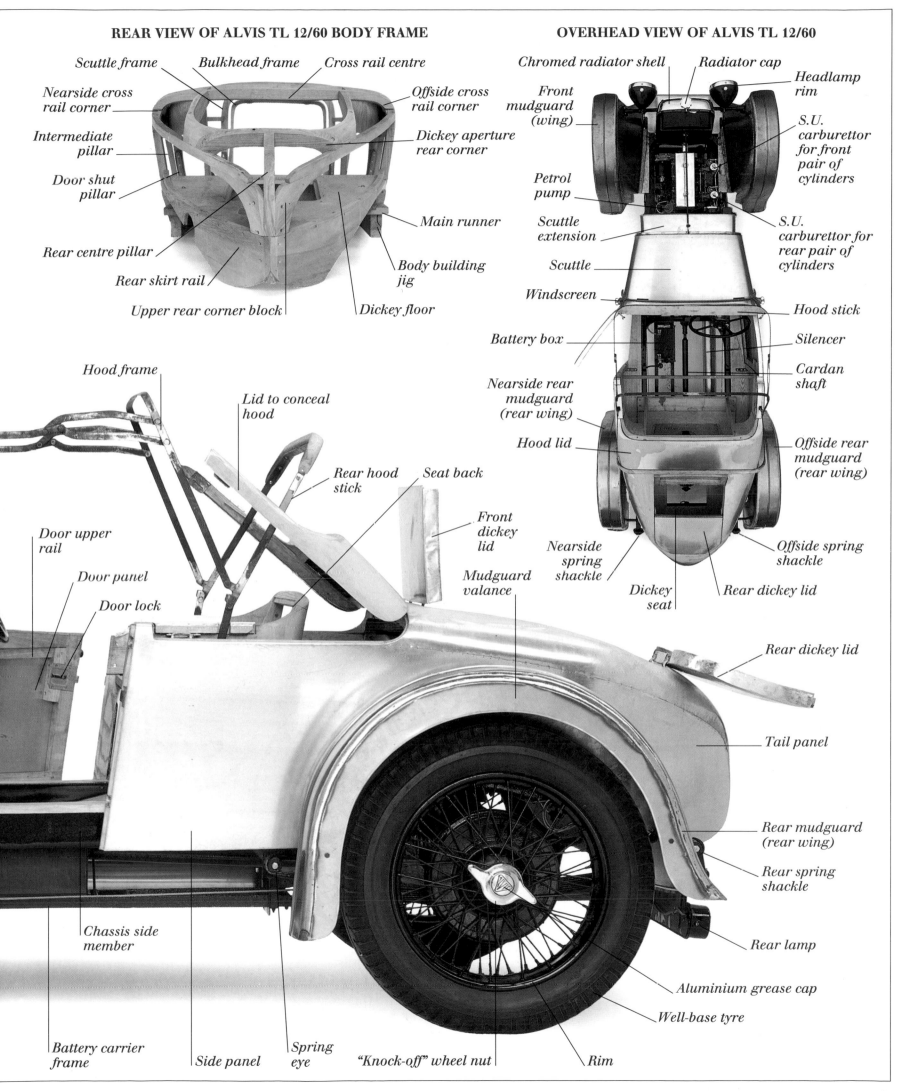

REAR VIEW OF ALVIS TL 12/60 BODY FRAME

Scuttle frame

Bulkhead frame

Cross rail centre

Nearside cross rail corner

Offside cross rail corner

Intermediate pillar

Dickey aperture rear corner

Door shut pillar

Rear centre pillar

Main runner

Rear skirt rail

Body building jig

Upper rear corner block

Dickey floor

OVERHEAD VIEW OF ALVIS TL 12/60

Chromed radiator shell

Radiator cap

Headlamp rim

Front mudguard (wing)

S.U. carburettor for front pair of cylinders

Petrol pump

S.U. carburettor for rear pair of cylinders

Scuttle extension

Scuttle

Windscreen

Hood stick

Battery box

Silencer

Cardan shaft

Nearside rear mudguard (rear wing)

Hood lid

Offside rear mudguard (rear wing)

Nearside spring shackle

Offside spring shackle

Dickey seat

Rear dickey lid

Hood frame

Lid to conceal hood

Rear hood stick

Seat back

Front dickey lid

Door upper rail

Mudguard valance

Door panel

Door lock

Rear dickey lid

Tail panel

Rear mudguard (rear wing)

Rear spring shackle

Chassis side member

Rear lamp

Aluminium grease cap

Battery carrier frame

Side panel

Spring eye

"Knock-off" wheel nut

Well-base tyre

Rim

Trim and upholstery

"TRIM" REFERS TO the embellishments of a car, such as the seats, windows, tyres, and decoration. "Upholstery" refers to the soft materials used. Cars reached a peak of ostentation with the American models of the 1950s, like the Cadillac Eldorado. Such cars often had large amounts of chrome-plated metalwork and extravagantly upholstered interiors; some even had gold-plated "brightwork" (polished metalwork). Although seats originally used horsehair and individually pocketed springs, they are now usually made with foam filling, which can be moulded to the required shape. Many luxury cars still use hand-stitched leather hides for their upholstery, and matched wood veneers to trim their dashboards and door cappings.

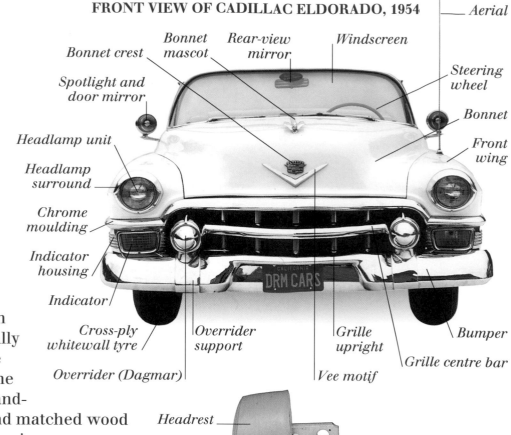

FRONT VIEW OF CADILLAC ELDORADO, 1954

Aerial · Bonnet crest · Bonnet mascot · Rear-view mirror · Windscreen · Steering wheel · Spotlight and door mirror · Bonnet · Headlamp unit · Front wing · Headlamp surround · Chrome moulding · Indicator housing · Indicator · Cross-ply whitewall tyre · Overrider (Dagmar) · Overrider support · Grille upright · Grille centre bar · Vee motif · Bumper

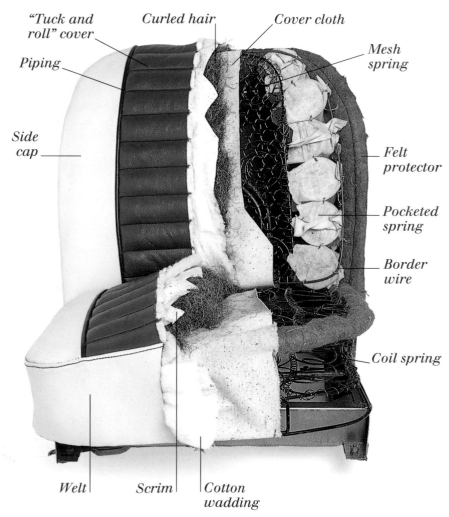

"Tuck and roll" cover · Curled hair · Cover cloth · Piping · Mesh spring · Side cap · Felt protector · Pocketed spring · Border wire · Coil spring · Welt · Scrim · Cotton wadding

SECTIONED TRADITIONAL SPRUNG SEAT

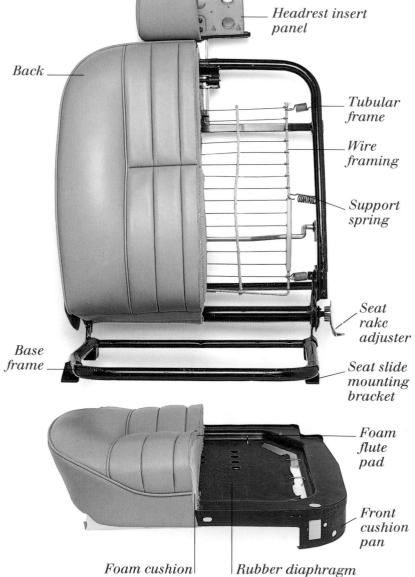

Headrest · Headrest insert panel · Back · Tubular frame · Wire framing · Support spring · Seat rake adjuster · Seat slide mounting bracket · Foam flute pad · Base frame · Foam cushion · Rubber diaphragm · Front cushion pan

SECTIONED MODERN SEAT

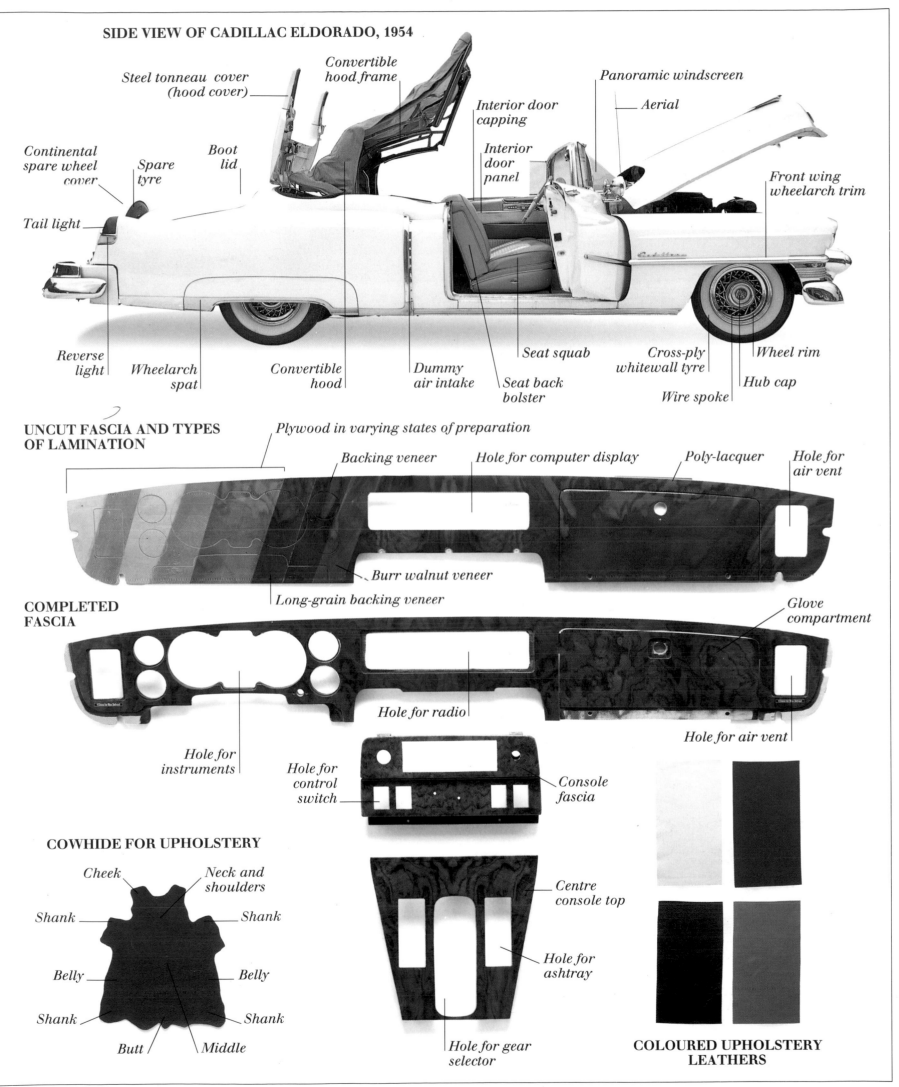

SIDE VIEW OF CADILLAC ELDORADO, 1954

Steel tonneau cover (hood cover)

Convertible hood frame

Panoramic windscreen

Aerial

Interior door capping

Continental spare wheel cover

Spare tyre

Boot lid

Interior door panel

Front wing wheelarch trim

Tail light

Reverse light

Wheelarch spat

Convertible hood

Dummy air intake

Seat back bolster

Seat squab

Cross-ply whitewall tyre

Wheel rim

Hub cap

Wire spoke

UNCUT FASCIA AND TYPES OF LAMINATION

Plywood in varying states of preparation

Backing veneer

Hole for computer display

Poly-lacquer

Hole for air vent

Burr walnut veneer

Long-grain backing veneer

COMPLETED FASCIA

Glove compartment

Hole for radio

Hole for air vent

Hole for instruments

Hole for control switch

Console fascia

COWHIDE FOR UPHOLSTERY

Cheek

Neck and shoulders

Shank

Shank

Belly

Belly

Shank

Shank

Butt

Middle

Centre console top

Hole for ashtray

Hole for gear selector

COLOURED UPHOLSTERY LEATHERS

All-terrain vehicles

THE MODERN ALL-TERRAIN VEHICLE has its origins in the US military Jeep of the 1940s and the British Land Rover. Such vehicles have been used for a wide range of purposes, from safari travel to fire-fighting. The principal special features of such cars – including four- or six-wheel drive, high ground clearance, and toughened braking, suspension, and transmission systems – are designed to enable driving under the most difficult off-road conditions. The vehicle shown here is equipped for safari travel and carries a comprehensive range of survival apparatus.

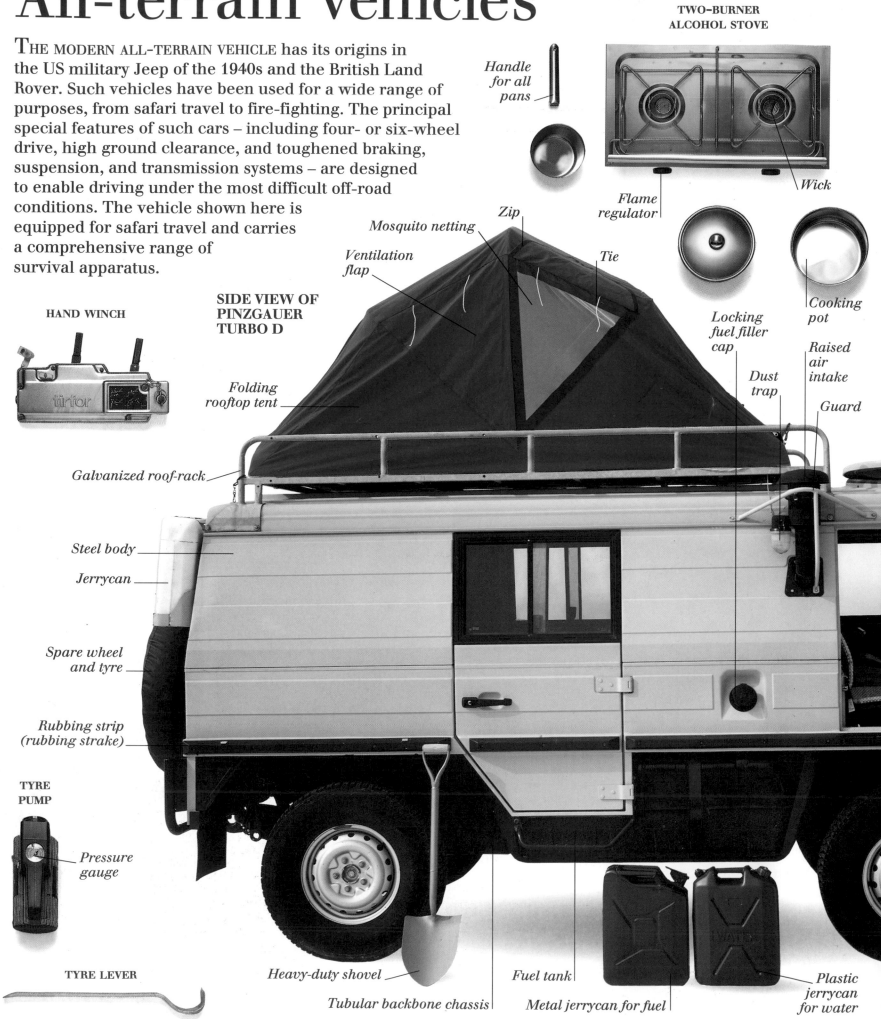

COOKING EQUIPMENT

TWO–BURNER ALCOHOL STOVE

Handle for all pans

Flame regulator

Wick

Cooking pot

HAND WINCH

SIDE VIEW OF PINZGAUER TURBO D

Zip

Mosquito netting

Ventilation flap

Tie

Folding rooftop tent

Locking fuel filler cap

Dust trap

Raised air intake

Guard

Galvanized roof-rack

Steel body

Jerrycan

Spare wheel and tyre

Rubbing strip (rubbing strake)

TYRE PUMP

Pressure gauge

TYRE LEVER

Heavy-duty shovel

Fuel tank

Tubular backbone chassis

Metal jerrycan for fuel

Plastic jerrycan for water

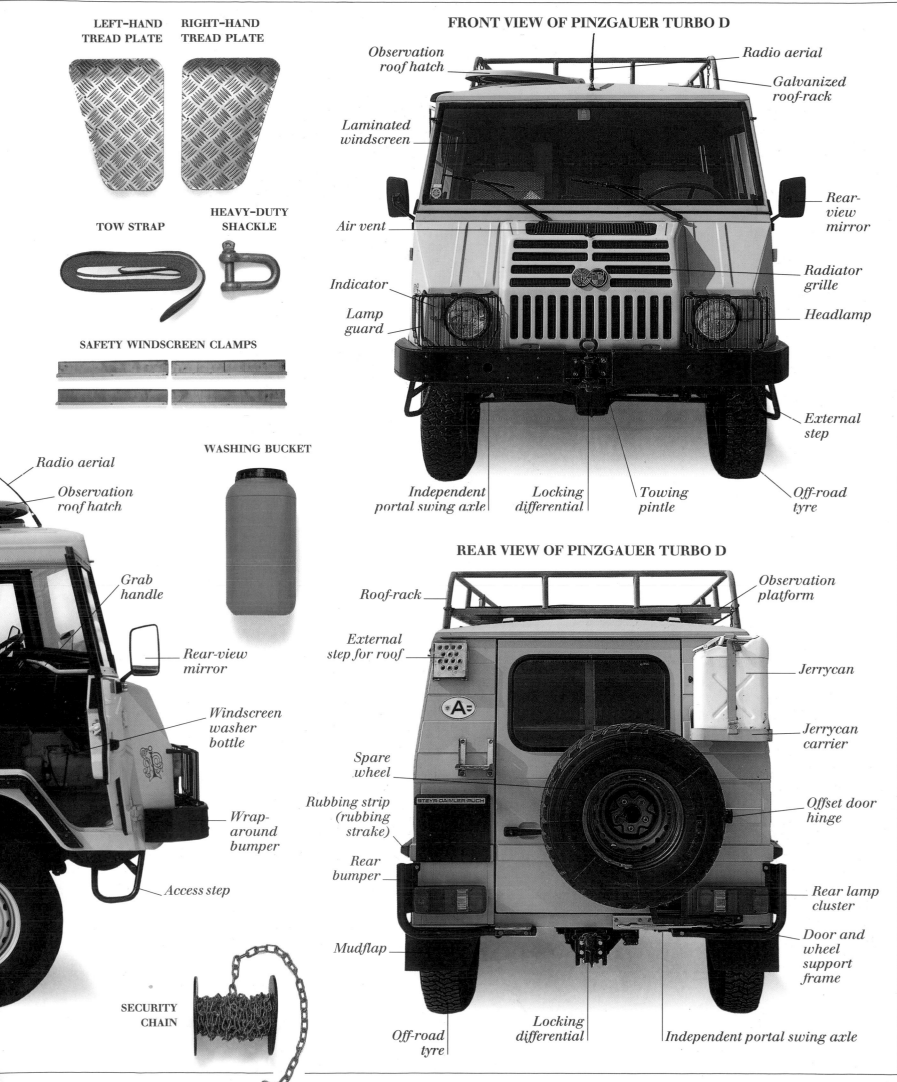

LEFT-HAND
TREAD PLATE

RIGHT-HAND
TREAD PLATE

TOW STRAP

HEAVY-DUTY
SHACKLE

SAFETY WINDSCREEN CLAMPS

Radio aerial

Observation
roof hatch

WASHING BUCKET

Grab
handle

Rear-view
mirror

Windscreen
washer
bottle

Wrap-
around
bumper

Access step

SECURITY
CHAIN

FRONT VIEW OF PINZGAUER TURBO D

Observation
roof hatch

Radio aerial

Galvanized
roof-rack

Laminated
windscreen

Rear-
view
mirror

Air vent

Indicator

Radiator
grille

Lamp
guard

Headlamp

External
step

Independent
portal swing axle

Locking
differential

Towing
pintle

Off-road
tyre

REAR VIEW OF PINZGAUER TURBO D

Roof-rack

Observation
platform

External
step for roof

Jerrycan

Jerrycan
carrier

Spare
wheel

Rubbing strip
(rubbing
strake)

Offset door
hinge

Rear
bumper

Rear lamp
cluster

Mudflap

Door and
wheel
support
frame

Off-road
tyre

Locking
differential

Independent portal swing axle

57

Racing cars

SINCE MOTORING BEGAN, racing cars have been a major focus of innovation in car design. Features that are now commonplace, such as disc brakes, turbochargers, and even safety belts, were used first on competition cars. Research into racing cars has contributed to a new understanding of engine performance, aerodynamics, and tyre adhesion, and has led to the development of ultra-light materials such as carbon-fibre for car bodies. Like the 1937 Bugatti Type 57S below, today's Williams Formula One car has a low, streamlined body and an open cockpit, but, unlike its forerunner, it also has a front wing that pushes the front wheels firmly on to the track, huge slick tyres for extra grip, and electrical sensors that continually relay information to the pits about the car's performance.

1937 BUGATTI TYPE 57S

Diffuser

Bodywork bracket

Heat shield

Forward radius arm

Rear wing upper mainplane

Slot

Upper flap

Half shaft

Rear radius arm

Temperature-sensitive sticker

Aeroquip pipe union

Oil tank

Constant velocity joint cover

Rear wing end-plate

Diffuser

Rear brake duct

Oil feed to engine

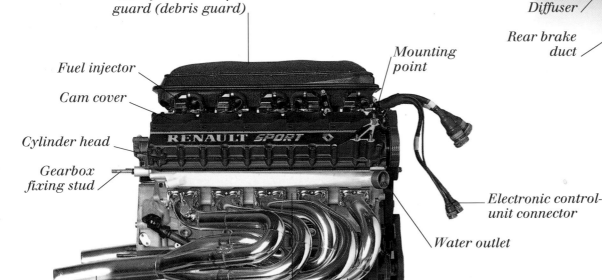

Fuel injection trumpet guard (debris guard)

Fuel injector

Cam cover

Cylinder head

Gearbox fixing stud

Mounting point

Electronic control-unit connector

Water outlet

Tail pipe

Stressed cylinder block

Harmonically-tuned exhaust pipe

RENAULT V10 RS1 ENGINE

ENGINE COWLING

Dzus fastener

Water
rail

Engine cooling
radiator

Master electrical
switch

Anchor
nut

Radiator
air duct

Slick
racing tyre

Steering
link

Nose
cover

Front wing
end-plate

Front
wing

Rear-view mirror

Suspension
push-rod

Lower wishbone

Front lower wishbone

Brake pipe

Driver's radio
aerial

Single-point
safety harness
release

Safety
harness

Upper
wishbone

Push-rod
adjuster

Electrical
connectors
to engine

Lifting
hook

Emergency air hose
for driver

Exhaust

Chassis
electrical
plug

Emergency
electricity
cut-off

Fuel filler

Fuel injection
air-intake trumpet

Fuel breather

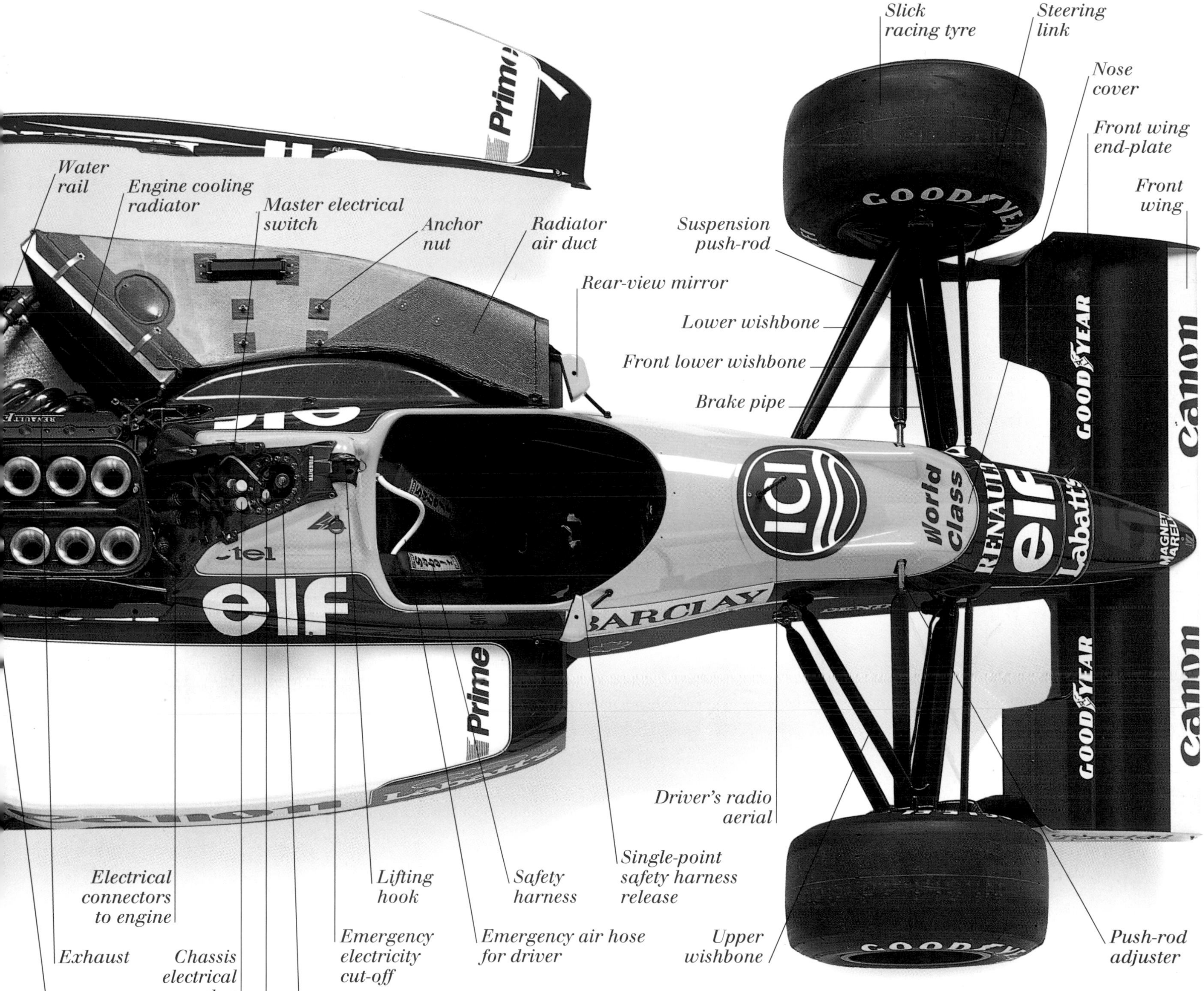

FRONT VIEW OF WILLIAMS 1990 FORMULA ONE RACING CAR

Rear wing upper
mainplane

Engine
air intake

Driver's radio aerial

Rear wing end-plate

Rear-view mirror

Upper
wishbone

Rear brake
duct

Suspension
push-rod

Slick racing tyre

Air
intake

Radiator
air intake

Steering link

Front wing

Front wing
end-plate

End-plate
aerodynamic skirt

Index

Acknowledgments

Dorling Kindersley would like to thank the following:
Signore Amadelli, Museo dell' Automobile Carlo Biscaretti di Ruffia, for the
Bordino Steam Carriage; Paul Bolton, Mazda MCL Group, for the Mazda RX-7
and the Wankel engine; Duncan Bradford of Reg Mills Wire Wheels, for the hub
and wire racing wheel; John and Leslie Brewster, Autocavan, for Beetle spares;
David Burgess-Wise, for the de Dion Bouton and Pilain clutch; Trevor Cass,
Garrett Turbo Service, for the turbocharger; John Corbett, The Patrick
Collection, for the Jaguar V12 engine; Gary Crumpler, Williams Grand Prix
Engineering Ltd, for the Grand Prix car and engine; Mollie Easterbrooke and
Duncan Gough, Overland Ltd, for the Pinzgauer Turbo D; Arthur Fairley,
Vauxhall Motor Company, for the digitized instrument panel; Paul
Foulkes-Halbard, Filching Manor Motor Museum, for the 70HP Mercedes and
the Oldsmobile; Frank Gilbert, I. Wilkinson and Son Ltd, for the Rolls-Royce
Silver Ghost "D" front limousine, the 1913 and 1924 Rolls-Royce Silver Ghost
Tourers, the Alvis TL 12/60, and the Lanchester chassis; Paolo Gratton, Gratton
Museum, for the Ford Model T; Colvin Gunn, of Gunn & Son, for the
supercharger; Judy Hogg of Ecurie Bertelli, for the Aston Martin; Milton

Holman, Dream Cars, for the Cadillac; Ian Matthews, IMAT Electronics, for
assistance; Eric Neal, Jaguar Cars Ltd, for the Jaguar engines, fascia, sectioned
seat, and running gear, and for general assistance; Paul Niblett, Keith Davidson,
Mark Reumel, and David Woolf, Michelin Tyre plc, for tyres and materials; Doug
Nye, for assistance; Kevin O'Keefe, O'Keefe Cars, for the electric seat; Seat UK, for
the Seat Ibiza; Roger Smith, for the Leyat; Jim Stirling, Ironbridge Gorge
Museum, for the wooden wheel; Jon Taylor, for the Beetle; Doug Thompson, for
the sprung seat; and Martyn Watkins, Ford Motor Company Ltd. In particular, for
invaluable assistance and the supply of many items for photography: The
National Motor Museum, Beaulieu; Alf Newell, Renault UK Ltd; David Suter,
Cheltenham Cutaway Exhibits Ltd; and Francesca Riccini, Science Museum.

Additional photography:
Michelangelo Gratton of Vision, Peter Chadwick, Dave King, Nick Parfitt.

Additional editorial assistance:
Roger Tritton, Fiona Courtney-Thompson, Deirdre Clark.